T0348525

Investigations
150 Things You Should Know

Investigations
150 Things You Should Know

Louis A. Tyska   Lawrence J. Fennelly

BUTTERWORTH
HEINEMANN

An Imprint of Elsevier

Boston   Oxford   Auckland   Johannesburg   Melbourne   New Delhi

Butterworth–Heinemann

An Imprint of Elsevier

Copyright © 1999 by Butterworth–Heinemann

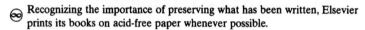A member of the Reed Elsevier group

All rights reserved.

No part of this publication may be reproduced, stored in a retrieval system, or transmitted in any form or by any means, electronic, mechanical, photocopying, recording, or otherwise, without the prior written permission of the publisher.

Permissions may be sought directly from Elsevier's Science and Technology Rights Department in Oxford, UK. Phone: (44) 1865 843830, Fax: (44) 1865 853333, e-mail: permissions@elsevier.co.uk. You may also complete your request on-line via the Elsevier homepage: http://www.elsevier.com by selecting "Customer Support" and then "Obtaining Permissions".

 Recognizing the importance of preserving what has been written, Elsevier prints its books on acid-free paper whenever possible.

Elsevier supports the efforts of American Forests and the Global ReLeaf program in its campaign for the betterment of trees, forests, and our environment.

Library of Congress Cataloging-in-Publication Data
Tyska, Louis A., 1934–
    Investigations : 150 things you should know / Louis A. Tyska and
Lawrence J. Fennelly.
        p.   cm.
    Includes bibliographical references.
    ISBN-13: 978-0-7506-7182-8   ISBN-10: 0-7506-7182-3 (pbk.: alk. paper)
    1. Private investigators—United States—Handbooks, manuals, etc.   2. Criminal investigation—United States—Handbooks, manuals, etc.   3. Investigations—United States—Handbooks, manuals, etc.   I. Fennelly, Lawrence J., 1940–   .   II. Title.
HV8093.T97   1999
363.25—dc21   99–12733
                                                                                                        CIP

British Library Cataloguing-in-Publication Data
A catalogue record for this book is available from the British Library.

The publisher offers special discounts on bulk orders of this book.
For information, please contact:
Manager of Special Sales
Elsevier
200 Wheeler Road, 6th Floor
Burlington, MA 01803
Tel: 781-313-4700
Fax: 781-313-4882
ISBN-13: 978-0-7506-7182-8
ISBN-10: 0-7506-7182-3 (pbk.: alk. paper)
For information on all Butterworth–Heinemann publications available, contact our World Wide Web home page at: http://www.bh.com

Transferred to Digital Printing, 2010

Printed and bound in the United Kingdom

Dedication

To both our families who have been, are, and always will be our focus. Through the good times and bad, we have all grown. We now pass it all on to Billy, Maggie, Jessica, Kayla, Kendra, and others who may join them.

Contents

Foreword

Many years ago, when first exposed to the field of investigations, some sage instructors imputed in us young students a number of salient points: (1) the purpose of an investigation is to resolve the allegation or complaint; (2) all crimes are solvable, one needs only to invest the manpower, money, material, methods, and machinery to arrive at the solution; and (3) at all crime scenes, the perpetrator either leaves something or takes away something that will link him/her with the crime. It is up to the skill of the investigator to find those pieces of evidence that puts a name with the criminal act. These gems of wisdom were spoken before the age of computers and when criminal laws affecting investigators were still relatively non-complex.

Since that time, laws changing on seemingly a daily basis, new technologies, and new techniques have all significantly impacted on the body of knowledge that an investigator must possess. Until now, there has been lacking within the investigative field one source document, one ready reference containing answers to questions investigators frequently need to know quickly. This book fills that void.

Investigations: 150 Things You Should Know will be just as valuable to the seasoned investigator as to the young student preparing to enter this career field. It belongs on the bookshelf of every Corporate Security Department, every college and university with a Criminal Justice or related course of study, and every private investigator. It is not your traditional book that you read in one sitting, but rather a resource, a ready reference that in a second will get or keep you on track for problem resolution. It is an ideal text to assist a public law enforcement officer at the city, state, or federal level, that will assist in transitioning to the private sector just as the subjects themselves transition from old time tested techniques of the 1950s to new information age technologies of the new millennium.

James P. Carino, Jr., CPP
Executive Director
Intelnet

Acknowledgments

To all the people who have contributed to our base of experience over the span of our careers, we are indebted. A special thanks to Debbie Lynch who labored with us over our notes and research and brought order to chaos. Over the years and through many efforts our editor, Laurel DeWolf, became our friend and the subject of our attempt at humor. Also, her sidekick at Butterworth–Heinemann, Rita Lombard, became ours as well. Finally, we want to acknowledge all of the authors and professionals who took time to take pen, pencil, or mouse in hand to write and thus share their knowledge and experience with us. We learned from you and hope to pass that on to those who follow us.

Louis A. Tyska
Lawrence J. Fennelly

1

Abandonment[1]

A person can have no expectation of privacy in property or items that have been abandoned. *Abandonment* means giving up something without limitation as to any particular person or purpose. Thus, if someone throws an object from a vehicle or leaves something behind in an abandoned vehicle, that evidence can be seized and used against the defendant in a criminal case.

2

Activities of the Detective[2]

A realistic view of investigative activities can be conveyed by describing how a typical case is handled, variations that frequently occur in the typical pattern, departmental policies that govern how cases are handled, and the supporting activities police perform to increase the likelihood of perpetrator identification and apprehension.

3

The Arraignment[3]

Normally, the arraignment takes place after an indictment or information is filed following a grand jury session or a preliminary hearing. At the arraignment, the judge informs the suspect of the charges against him or her. The accused has a constitutional right at this stage of the process to be informed of the nature and the cause of the accusations. The judge accomplishes this by reading the formal charge document—the complaint, the information, or the indictment—to the accused. The judge also appoints counsel, if counsel has not yet been retained by the defendant. The judge must ensure that the accused understands the charges and is competent to stand trial. After the charges are read and explained, the defendant is asked to enter a plea. If the plea is "not guilty," a trial date is set.

One of the principles underlying American jurisprudence is that the suspect is morally and legally entitled to make a plea of not guilty. Usually this is the suspect's first chance to plead and declare his innocence. And when a plea of not guilty is entered, the burden is on the state to prove beyond a reasonable doubt all the charges against the defendant.

If the accused enters a plea of guilty during the arraignment, he or she surrenders a number of constitutional rights—for example, the rights to silence, to confront witnesses, to a trial by jury, and so forth. Consequently, before a plea of guilty will be accepted by the court, certain conditions must be met. The plea must be entered voluntarily, and the defendant must be aware of the implications of the plea. A guilty plea is considered equivalent to a verdict of guilty. The court may deliver a sentence at the time of the plea or set a date for sentencing.

Before the judge accepts the plea, however, he or she must be convinced that the defendant has made a voluntary and intelligent plea of guilty. Often there is a conversation between the judge and the defendant for the judge to determine these facts. This conversation is often referred to as the *plea colloquy*. If the judge is satisfied, the defendant is scheduled for sentencing; if not, the judge can refuse to consider the guilty plea and enter a plea of not guilty for the defendant into the record, set a trial date, and demand that the defendant stand trial.

The U.S. Supreme Court has ruled that "when a guilty plea rests in any significance on the promise or an agreement of the prosecutor, so it can be said to be part of the inducement or consideration, such promise must be fulfilled" (*Santobello v. New York*, 1971). Hence, when a guilty plea is given to a judge, he or she is mandated to ask a certain series of questions to ensure that the method by which the plea bargain was reached adheres to the principles dictated by the Court. Around the courthouse, this series of questions is referred to as the "copping out ceremony."

4

Arrest and Detention: 21 Things You Should Know[4]

The following points serve as evaluative tools by which protection professionals can assess detention practices:

1. Know and articulate the specific purpose of detention—self-defense, recovery of merchandise, protection of others, prevention of trespass, and so forth. Officers should be able to unequivocally state why they are restricting someone's freedom.
2. Have a written policy on detention that is implemented via specific procedures and post orders.
3. Develop a policy after assessing state statutes, regulatory requirements, case law, and local law enforcement agency procedures.
4. Know the policy and operating procedures of responding law enforcement agencies.
5. Call police as soon as possible in those cases requiring their assistance—for example, when persons are violent and/or where criminal charges will be brought against someone.
6. Record the times of calls to the police, the results of such calls, and the arrival times, numbers, and names of responding police officers.
7. Use effective and legally correct (truthful, accurate) verbalization when detaining.
8. Tell the detainee what is transpiring but give no more information than is necessary. Provide a basic explanation, but do not engage in protracted dialogue about the reason, the officer's authority, and so forth. Lengthy discussions create room for argument!
9. Be as polite and considerate as possible to the detainee. Scrupulously avoid referring to them in demeaning terms.

10. Assess the detainee and environment for safety—avoid areas with a lot of glass, easy access to weapons, hazardous materials, or areas that cannot be secured from associates of the detainee—before initiating the contact.
11. Avoid physical contact and document in detail any and all physical contact that occurs.
12. Understand the relationship of the detainee to your employer as much as possible. An employee can be spoken to longer in the eyes of the courts as they are being compensated for their time via an established business relationship.
13. Detain in a safe, secure area under your control. Control is the issue. Whose "turf" the detention occurs on will play a large role in determining this.
14. Detain in a private place. A quiet, somewhat secluded, comfortable office environment is best to minimize interpersonal tensions between the officer and detainee. A private setting also helps to preclude any embarrassment the detainee may feel.
15. Have witnesses to the detention who are the same sex as the detainee.
16. Search the detainee in an appropriate manner: visual scan, cursory search for weapons, consent search of purse. Employer policies will dictate the type and nature of the search. Officers should always have some reasonable degree of assurance that the detainee is not armed.
17. Restrain the detainee in an appropriate manner; have them sit with hands in view, handcuff them, use four-position restraints.
18. Separate detainees from each other.
19. Question detainees for basic information and record their statements.
20. Debrief the detainee as appropriate by complimenting them, explaining the impropriety to them, or getting their acknowledgement of their inappropriate actions.
21. Document the detention completely, being sure to include all statements, admissions, and threats.

5

Arrest by Private Citizens[5]

Private citizens may make arrests under certain and varying conditions in specific jurisdictions. Fourth Amendment sanctions apply to sworn police and may apply to those who are commissioned, deputized, or licensed. Normal requirements for police to make an arrest include probable cause, that is, reasonable grounds that a crime has been or is being committed. Note that the requirements for some states include the restriction that a felony in fact has been committed. This requirement is more stringent than probable cause or reasonable grounds. Note the differences in various jurisdictions. Presence is a requirement in most jurisdictions. Making an unreasonable arrest or invalid detention subjects the arrestor or detainor to intentional tort lawsuits such as false arrest/imprisonment and assault and battery. Knowledge of the exact arrest requirements to prevent loss from lawsuit is a necessity for security employees.

BACKGROUND

Private persons have long had the authority to make *citizens arrests*. The questions are: For what crimes can a private person make an arrest? Under what conditions can the arrest be made? What are the requirements for making the arrest good?

The authority is derived in some states by statute and in other states by common law. While the same general theme applies on a nationwide basis, the reader should remember that different states may have their own "spin" on the general theme. One should also be familiar with the various state interpretations of the statutes. Note how English common law was made into a statute in this case and how case law interpreted the phrase "certain information" that came from the statute.

6

Arrest Tactics[6]

When law enforcement officers make an arrest, particularly a felony arrest, the potential for violence exists. To reduce the possibility of injury or death of anyone involved, it is essential to prepare for any foreseeable consequences. At a minimum, attempt to determine the floor plan of the structure where the suspect is thought to be in order to enter as quickly and effectively as possible. Planning should include a discussion of:

- Equipment needed, such as raid jackets, ram, weapons, flashlights, body armor, and first aid kits
- Where the suspect will be taken after the arrest
- What to do with third parties, such as a spouse and children
- Where the closest medical facilities are located

7

Arson

Arson by definition[7] is the

> Willful and malicious setting fire to, or causing to be burned, or aiding, counseling or procuring the burning of, a dwelling house, or building adjoining or adjacent to a dwelling house, or a building by the burning whereof a dwelling house is burned, whether such dwelling house or other building is the property of himself or another and whether the same is occupied or unoccupied.

ELEMENTS OF ARSON

1. Malicious intent
2. Set fire or burn certain buildings
3. Aiding in such burning

RELATED STATUTES

- Burning of nonresidential buildings, railway cars, ships, and vessels
- Burning of wood, fences, corn, grain, trees, motor vehicles
- Attempted arson
- Burning insured property with intent to defraud
- Burning insured motor vehicles, no payment until report filed with appropriate fire department

PROFILING THE ARSONIST

Motives for arson include financial (to defraud one's insurance company), revenge, concealing another crime, destroying corporate records, sabotage, murder, extortion, intimidation, the amateur thrill seeker or attention seeker, sexual perversion, and/or vandalism.

Some facts about fire and arson:

1. Fire department administration have been successful for several years with mutual aid programs.
2. Fire is the number one cause of property damage and destruction.
3. Most deaths caused by fire are as a result of smoke and heat.

8

Body Language, Body Movement, and Body Signs[8]

BODY MOVEMENT	POSSIBLE MEANING
Head and Face:	
Lowering the eyebrows	Concentration or anger
Raised eyebrows	Surprise or anticipation
Widening of eyes	High interest or fear
Removing of glasses	Withdrawal
Closing nostrils with fingers	Contempt
Index finger along side of nose	Suspicion
Mouth falls open	Boredom or Unsure of self
Flared nostrils	Aggression/Hatred
Cheeks sucked in	Disapproval/critical attitude
Tongue flicking teeth	Sexually aggressive
Biting lips	Self-deprecation
Lowering chin and looking up	Coy or shy
Picking face or biting nails	Unsure, negative feelings

continued

BODY MOVEMENT	POSSIBLE MEANING
Hands and Arms:	
Fingering collar of shirt	Nervous/desire to escape
Hand over heart or middle of chest	Honesty
Playing unconsciously with ring	Possible conflict
Wiping under nose with finger	Aggression
Drumming or tapping fingers	Impatience, hostility, frustration
Fingers steepled	Superiority
Hands held behind head	Confident, superiority
Male running fingers through hair	Uncertainty
Female playing with hair	Flirtation
Folding hands deep in lap	Defense against rejection
Self scratching, picking, squeezing	Aggression, hostility
Woman exposing palm to man	Flirtation
Rubbing objects	Reassurance, sensuousness
Fist clenching or pounding	Aggression
Hand covering face	Protection, concealment
Covering eyes with hands	Fear or shame

9

The Burden of Proof at a Criminal Trial[9]

All prosecution evidence in a criminal trial must present a standard of proof that is higher than in any other trial in the American system of justice. As we saw previously, the standard of proof is that of guilt beyond a reasonable doubt. No defendant may be convicted in this country during the adjudicatory stage of the criminal process without the prosecution meeting this burden of proof. The reasonable doubt standard is the fundamental legal principle of the American criminal justice system. It is viewed as the essential instrument for lessening the risk of conviction based on factual errors (see following table). The U.S. Supreme Court has announced in many decisions that it is better to release 100 guilty persons than to convict someone who is innocent.

Standard	Definition	Where Used
Absolute certainty	No possibility of error; 100 percent certainty	Not used in civil or criminal law
Beyond reasonable doubt; moral certainty	Conclusive and complete proof, while leaving any reasonable doubt as to the innocence or guilt of the defendant; allowing the defendant the benefit of any possibility of innocence	
Clear and convincing evidence	Prevailing and persuasive to the trier of fact	Civil commitments, insanity defense
Preponderance of evidence	Greater weight of evidence in terms of credibility; more convincing than an opposite point of view	Civil trial
Probable cause	U.S. constitutional standard for arrest and search warrants, requiring existence of facts sufficient to warrant that a crime has been committed	Arrest, preliminary hearing, motions
Sufficient evidence	Adequate evidence to reverse a trial court	Appellate review
Reasonable suspicion	Rational, reasonable belief that facts warrant investigation of a crime on less than probable cause	Police investigations
Less than probable	Mere suspicion; less than reasonable to conclude criminal activity exists	Prudent police investigation where safety of an officer or others is endangered

10

Cargo Theft Investigative Techniques

Investigative techniques that can be employed to investigate cargo thefts are limited only by one's imagination. Repeated use of new techniques will enable investigators to become more proficient. Tried and true techniques will always remain in an investigator's bag of tricks.

Some investigative techniques include, but are not limited to following:

1. Informants

Although informants were previously discussed as a source of information, the cultivating of informants is an important investigative technique. Informants' personalities vary, as do their motivations. An investigator must be constantly aware of informants' personality traits and motivations without losing sight of the object of the investigation. This can best be accomplished by appropriate direction and control of an informant by the investigator. Informants who come from a cargo related background are diverse.

2. Undercover Investigation

For many investigators, this is the most popular investigative technique. However, selection of an investigator for an undercover assignment is critical. Cargo situations demand specific needs from an investigator such as knowledge of cargo handling, suitable appearance and physical make up, and possession of a specific mindset.

3. Surveillance

With the increased mobility of the criminal element, surveillance techniques have expanded from the traditional vehicle and foot to include air, vessel, and hardware. Foot, vehicle, air, and vessel surveillance involve separate skills. Proficiency is acquired only through extensive participation in each type of surveillance.

4. Use of Technical Equipment

Technical aids which, when properly used, can greatly assist the investigator in his investigation include:

- Electronic sensors and devices
- Photography
- Fluorescent powders

- Night vision and infrared scopes
- Closed circuit television with videotape time sequences.

5. Telephone Number Analysis
Internal and company generated telephone data may be reviewed to determine patterns of activity and possible internal conspirators. A computer system is available for producing reports from toll data in which the information is sorted chronologically and numerically by telephone. This system can be extremely helpful in solidifying cargo theft conspiracy cases that have internal company involvement.

6. Identify "Fence" Operations
Cargo thefts would be greatly reduced if the thief did not have a readily available outlet to buy the merchandise. Fence operations are directly and indirectly connected with organized crime. Fencing operations vary. In many instances, they operate legitimate businesses or warehouses, but their fencing operations are carried out clandestinely. In recent years, flea markets and swap shops have become a distribution point for fences.

To identify fences, investigators work undercover and make larger and larger purchases of stolen merchandise. This technique may enable an investigation to proceed in an upward direction in an effort to identify other individuals involved in a theft organization or redistribution process.

7. Storefront Operations
By identifying fences and making purchases, a certain amount of expertise in this area is gained. The knowledge of a fencing operation and the argot used between a thief and a fence will be of great help when a storefront project is undertaken by public or private enforcements. Storefront operations are time consuming, expensive, and extremely hazardous, but the payoffs are great when the need for such operations has been identified.

8. Fraudulent Cargo Documentation
Detecting practices involving fraudulent papers and other forms of misrepresentations that facilitate cargo thefts is a technique that should be developed. Knowledge of documents required for the importation and movement of cargo to its ultimate destination and the authenticity of those documents can disclose fraudulent practices. As soon as fraudulent documentation is used to steal cargo, the authorities should be alerted. The thieves may become aware that their method of operation has been discovered; however, prevention of future thefts is most important.

11

Cargo Theft Reporting:
14 Things You Should Do

All reported cargo thefts should be documented. Efforts should be made to determine the extent of investigation required. Some cases of reported theft involve losses so small that investigation, or at least extensive inquiry, may not be warranted. However, investigation of pilferage of even low-value merchandise from security enclosures within bonded premises may be warranted in most cases, since such thefts indicate breakdown of strict controls set up to protect those enclosures where high-value, low-bulk cargo presents an ideal target for thieves. Records are the backbone of an investigation and any effective prevention program.

Every reported theft should be documented. A report prepared in connection with a formal investigation should completely identify the shipment of merchandise and that portion stolen. An indication of actual or estimated retail value should be included in the report. Every effort should be made to include in the report the following information concerning the merchandise.

1. Name of importing vessel, vehicle or aircraft
2. Date and time of arrival of conveyance
3. Foreign port of lading, if appropriate
4. Bill of lading number or airway bill number
5. Identify foreign shipper and/or manufacturer
6. Identify customs broker (if applicable)
7. Name and identity of ultimate consignee
8. Carton and/or serial numbers of stolen merchandise (and other identifying marks or numbers)
9. Estimated retail value of stolen merchandise
10. Indicate whether stolen merchandise is imported or exported
11. Name and identification of person discovering theft
12. Location of apparent theft
13. Date and time theft discovered
14. Date theft was reported to authorities and to whom

Identification data for individuals and vehicles who are suspect in the investigation also should be included in the report.

12

Cargo Documentation Investigations

The movement of cargo is accompanied by documentation from the time it leaves the exporter's premises until it is received by the consignee. To conduct a meaningful investigation, it is necessary to understand the paper flow and the part played by each segment of the industry. Knowledge of general procedures and local differences in these procedures will be extremely beneficial in determining where a theft may have occurred, whether fraudulent documentation was used, and if collusion took place between various elements within the industry.

MARINE CARGO

1. The *steamship company* (or agent) receives via mail a copy of the vessel's cargo manifest. Normally, the consignee is notified two days prior to the ship's arrival. The carrier provides freight release to the terminal operator.

2. The *Customs broker* or consignee obtains freight release, Department of Agriculture clearance, and so forth before contacting the motor carrier. The broker forwards to the motor carrier an original of the domestic bill of lading and an original of the pickup order, which authorizes pick up of the cargo. It is the broker's responsibility to check the bill of lading for completeness and guarantee with the terminal operator the loading charges and demurrage.

3. The *motor carrier* secures an interchange agreement with a steamship company on containers and ascertains expiration of free time and availability of cargo for pick up before dispatching the driver for the pier. The motor carrier furnishes the driver with the original and a copy of the pick up order before his departure for the pier. An appointment is made with the terminal operator at least 24 hours before pick up. Within port movements of bonded shipments (warehouse or general order) require a motor carrier to be a customhouse license holder and require the truckmen to possess customs cartmen identification cards. When bonded shipments are authorized to be transported by common or private carriers, the identification cards are *not* required.

4. The *terminal operator* issues a pass to the driver at the gatehouse. The pick up order is checked for completeness and legibility by the terminal

operator dispatcher. The motor carrier's credit rating for loading charges is verified and arrangements made for payment of demurrage, if any. Unless cargo has been authorized for delivery to the steamship company by Customs, the terminal operator directs the driver to the pier Customs office.

5.   The *Customs inspector* will verify the driver's papers against prelodged Customs entry documents. When all Customs requirements are completed, the inspector will stamp the delivery order "Delivery Authorized."

6.   The *terminal operator* will notify the driver to load and assign a checker and loading area. The cargo is then loaded onto the vehicle by pier personnel and the checker notes exceptions and shortages.

It is at this point (with inbond entries only) that the joint determination between the checker, acting as the agent of the carrier, and driver, acting as the agent of the importer, present a joint determination to the Customs inspector. If there are any discrepancies, the inspector makes appropriate notations on all copies of the inbond documents, indicating that the joint determination was submitted. The inspector's notation does not affirm or deny the count, it only acknowledges the joint determination and the amount that is permitted. The original delivery order is retained by the terminal operator.

7.   It is the *driver's* responsibility to assist in and/or supervise the loading of his vehicle. He signs the delivery order for the quantity received and exceptions and shortages are noted, and retains a copy of the delivery order. Upon departure from the pier, he surrenders the gate pass at the gatehouse. Prior to leaving the pier, the driver notifies the motor carrier dispatcher that he has picked up the cargo and is proceeding with the delivery.

AIR CARGO

1.   Upon arrival, an aircraft is given clearance by Public Health and commences to unload its cargo. The *airline* checks the shipment against airway bills and notifies the consignee within 24 hours subsequent to arrival.

2.   The *Customs broker* or the consignee prepares the entry. The broker forwards to the inland carrier an original of the airway bill and an original of the pick up order, which authorizes the cargo to be picked up.

3.   The *Customs officer* will review all documents and upon examination will authorize delivery of the shipment to the carrier. The Customs inspector may designate a portion of the shipment to be held for appraisal.

4.   The *air cargo terminal operator* will examine the pick up order presented by the motor carrier and check it for completeness. If the cargo has not been authorized for delivery by Customs, the motor carrier must obtain this authorization prior to loading.

5. Upon loading of an inbond shipment, the *driver* and *airline representative* will make a joint determination and submit the results on the delivery order to Customs. All imported cargo arriving in the United States, other than noncommercial merchandise carried on the person by a traveler, is temporarily in the custody of the United States Customs Service until the importer or his authorized agent complies with whatever Customs requirements apply. Duty free, noncommercial importations may be cleared to the importer with little or no formality. Whenever formality is involved in the Customs transaction, authorizing delivery of the merchandise to the importer is referred to as an *entry*. Basically, there are three classes of entry: (1) transportation inbond, (2) consumption, and (3) warehouse.

Inbond Entries

1. Immediate Transportation (I.T.): This type of entry is used when merchandise arrives at one port, and is released on condition that it be transported inbond to another port. Upon arrival, Customs once again takes temporary custody until an entry of another type is filed by the importer.
2. Transportation and Exportation (T. & E.): This entry is used when merchandise may be merely passing through the United States to another country. The merchandise is permitted on condition that it be transported inbond out of the United States. Other entries of this type are temporary importation bond and permanent exhibition entry.

Consumption Entries

1. Informal Consumption Entries: These entries are allowed for commercial importations under specified value limits and for noncommercial importations regardless of value.
2. Formal Consumption Entries: At the time a formal consumption entry is filed, the importer pays whatever duties are due on the merchandise. After the shipment is examined and authorized for delivery by Customs, the importer can dispose of the merchandise as he wishes.
3. Immediate Delivery Procedure (I.D.)—Pending Formal or Informal Entries: This procedure is used to expedite the clearance of cargo. It allows up to ten days for the payment of estimated duty and processing of the commercial entry. In addition, it permits delivery of the cargo prior to payment of estimated duties and allows subsequent filing of the entry.

Warehouse Entries

The use of this type of entry allows the importer to hold his merchandise in a bonded Customs warehouse ready for sale and distribution, but does not have to pay Customs duty until he withdraws the merchandise from the warehouse.

13

Cargo: Air and Marine Documentation

The movement of goods by air or sea requires proper formal and informal documentation from the time it exits the shipper's facility until it is received by the consignee. To conduct an investigation you must understand the flow of documentation in each segment of movement. Understanding general procedures and any local variances can be helpful in determining where a theft occurred, whether fraudulent documentation was used, and if collusion took place.

MARINE CARGO

1.   The steamship authority or its agent receives a copy of the vessel's manifest either electronically or via mail or messenger. The consignees of the various shipments are usually notified at least two days prior to the ship's arrival. The carrier provides a freight release to the terminal operator.

2.   The consignee or the Customs broker obtains the freight release and such clearances as are required by law and then contacts the truckmen. The broker forwards to the truckman an original of the domestic bill of lading and an original of the pick up order that authorizes the pick up of the cargo. It is the broker's responsibility to check the documentation for completeness, accuracy and any charges required.

3.   The truckman obtains an interchange agreement with the steamship company in the case of containers. They determine the availability of the cargo prior to dispatching a driver for pick up. The driver has an original and one copy of the pick up order.

4.   The terminal operator issues a pass to the driver when he presents himself at the terminal. This is the first clearance location for the driver who is then to report to the United States Custom office at the terminal in the case of international cargo.

5.   United States Customs verifies the driver's papers against prelogged United States Customs entry documents. When all obligations for duties and/or charges are satisfied, Customs will authorize delivery.

6.   The terminal operator will load the driver with the authorized cargo. Any notations, such as exceptions or shortages, are noted by the load checker assigned by the terminal. It is at this juncture that there is a joint determination between the checker as the agent for the carrier and the truckman as the agent for the importer or consignee, as to the accuracy of the pick up. The original delivery order remains with the terminal operator.

7.   It is the truckman's responsibility to assist in and supervise the loading of his truck. He signs the delivery order for the quantity and condition of goods received. Any exceptions or violations are noted on the copy of the delivery order that he keeps. Upon departure from the terminal, the truckman surrenders the pass at exit.

AIR CARGO

1.   Upon arrival, an aircraft is given clearance by Public Health and commences to unload its cargo. The airline checks the shipment against airway bills and notifies the consignee within 24 hours subsequent to arrival.

2.   The Customs broker or the consignee prepares the entry. The broker forwards to the inland carrier an original of the airway bill and an original of the pick up order that authorizes the cargo to be picked up.

3.   The Customs officer will review all documents and upon examination will authorize delivery of the shipment to the carrier. The Customs inspector may designate a portion of the shipment to be held for appraisal.

4.   The air cargo terminal operator will examine the pick up order presented by the motor carrier and check it for completeness. If the cargo has not been authorized for delivery by Customs, the motor carrier must obtain this authorization prior to loading.

5.   Upon loading of an inbond shipment, the driver and airline representative will make a joint determination and submit the results on the delivery order to United States Customs.

NOTE: All imported cargo arriving in the United States, other than noncommercial merchandise carried on the person by a traveler, is temporarily in the custody of the U.S. Customs Service until the importer or his authorized agent complies with whatever Customs requirements apply. Duty free, noncommercial importations may be cleared to the importer with little or no formality. Whenever formality is involved, merchandise to the importer is referred to as an *entry*.

14

Checklist: Arson

- Who first noticed the fire?
- Who called in the fire?
- What color were the flames and smoke?
- Was there any kind of explosion before the fire?
- How did the fire start or ignite?
- Were any suspicious or unusual conditions or circumstances noted?
- Was anyone injured or killed?
- Who had access to the site?
- Was the owner of the property identified and interviewed?
- What is the amount of insurance and name of company?
- Is there an inventory of what was destroyed in the fire?
- Who took photos and videos of the fire scene?
- What personnel and fire equipment responded to the scene?
- Was the state Fire Marshall's office notified and who responded?
- Was available evidence collected and safeguarded?
- Were witnesses identified and interviewed?
- Coordinate a debriefing of authorities of those who responded, insurance representatives, and others as appropriate.

15

Checklist: Burglary

- What is the location and description of the burglarized facility?
- What were the time, date, and circumstances of the burglary? Was entry forced? If so, how?

- Is there a description and quantities of items taken, if any, by rightful owner?
- What were the exact location(s) of items taken?
- Was any physical evidence left at scene?
- Were there any witnesses? How was the burglary reported and by whom?
- Interview the owner for information concerning access, recent visitors or vendors, and the potential for fraud.
- Did you disseminate a description of the stolen goods or materials? Are any serial numbers or identifying marks or notations available?
- Was there a review of surrounding areas for similar types of burglaries?
- Describe the modus operandi, or MO, of the burglar(s). Type of entry, method of search of the premises, means of exit, time of day, items not taken are some of the pattern indicators to record and compare.

DEFINITION OF BURGLARY

Breaking and entering of the dwelling of another in the nighttime with intent to commit a felony.

ELEMENTS OF BURGLARY

1. Breaking
2. Entry
3. Dwelling
4. Of another
5. Nighttime
6. Felonious intent

RELATED STATUTES

Not all of the statutory crimes of breaking and entering contain all elements of common law burglary.

Burglary, not being armed

Burglary, being armed or making an assault

Breaking and entering building, ship, vessel or vehicle with intent to commit a misdemeanor

Breaking in nighttime, building, vehicle or ship: injury or destruction of safe or other depository of valuables

Entering in the nighttime without breaking, or in the daytime by breaking and entering, with intent to commit a felony, and causing the person lawfully therein to be put in fear

Entering dwelling house in nighttime or breaking, etc., without putting in fear in daytime with intent to commit a felony

Breaking and entering railroad car, and so forth

Making, holding, using, burglarious instruments or motor vehicle master keys

16

Checklist: Notification of Finding a Victim

- Who found the victim? What was the time and date? Were authorities notified, and what authorities were notified?
- What was the condition of the victim?
- Was there any medical response and by whom?
- If the victim was transported to a hospital or emergency care facility, by whom and to what facility?
- If there was a fatality, was there a statement or dying declaration taken?
- Who made observation of the scene and victim? Were observations recorded or documented?
- Was the victim or deceased identified? By whom or how?
- If deceased, was the cause identifiable? Recorded or described?
- What evidence was found, if any?
- Were any weapons or other pertinent material(s) found?
- Were there any witnesses?
- Were witnesses interviewed/debriefed and statements taken?
- Was evidence safeguarded for or by authorities? Was it properly collected, marked, and transported?
- Were photographs, sketches, and/or videos of the scene taken?
- Were suspects identified? Have descriptions been released?
- Have media concerns been addressed?

17

Checklist: Pedophile Investigations

- Identify the specific law(s) which have been broken.
- Have all elements of the law(s) been met?
- Have perpetrator(s) been identified and alibis verified?
- Is there a register of witnesses, if any, and synopsis of their knowledge of the crime(s)?
- Is all evidence identified, marked, tested, preserved, inventoried, and safeguarded?
- Is there a list of persons interviewed and summary of their contribution?
- Were statements taken verbally and/or written?
- Were photographs or videos of the pertinent concerns associated with the crime taken and catalogued with details relevant to the scene noted?
- Have applications for search and/or arrest warrants been made based upon probable cause?
- Acquire documented information supplied by the child/children, if possible. Note that details of time, date, and number of incidents are sometimes difficult to obtain.
- Provide support for concerns that without immediate action taken by authorities, abuse, mistreatment, or sexual assault may continue.
- Make notifications to appropriate welfare organizations including cooperation and sharing of history.
- Are there recommendations for eliminating or preventing continued offenses?
- Have media concerns been addressed?
- Is there protection for identities of all underage victims and/or witnesses?

18

Checklist: Robbery Investigations

- Was the facility alarmed and in working order?
- Was the alarm silent or forceful? Was there unauthorized entry?
- Was a response capability associated with the alarm?
- Are there sketches of high value areas or facilities on file with the response team or authorities?
- Is there a time lapse CCTV capability present and is it working?
- If the robbed facility was staffed, were individuals interviewed and debriefed?
- Are there written statements of victims and witnesses?
- Are there descriptions of the perpetrator(s) clothing, physical description, manner of speech, identifying marks or traits?
- Were any weapons observed or suspected?
- Were there any threats or actual assaults made?
- How did the perpetrator(s) exit the facility and effect their getaway?
- Was the facility searched for physical evidence? Was it recorded and inventoried?
- Were photographs, sketches, or videos taken?
- Were all the items taken in the robbery inventoried and descriptions and values noted?
- Was the legal owner present or notified?
- Were appropriate authorities notified; as in a bank robbery, was FBI notified?

DEFINITION OF ROBBERY

By force and violence, or by assault and putting in fear, robbing, stealing and taking from the person of another money or other property which may be the subject of larceny.

ELEMENTS OF ROBBERY

1. Larcency
2. From the person of another
3. By force and violence or by putting in fear

NOTE: By judicial interpretation, taking from the "person" includes taking from the victim's presence, which covers the situation where the victim, if not put in fear, could have prevented the taking (*Commonwealth v. Stewart*).

RELATED STATUTES

Robbery, armed

Robbery while masked

Robbery, unarmed

Reporting violent crimes; robbery, failure to report

Stealing by confining or putting in fear

Attempted extortion

Assault with intent to rob, not being armed

Confining or putting in fear for the purpose of stealing

19

Clearance and Arrest[10]

A major demand on an investigator's time occurs when a suspect is taken into custody—usually as a consequence of patrol activity. When an arrest occurs, an effort is made to clear similar crimes if possible by linking them to the arrested suspect. This responsibility falls to the investigator. If the suspect is willing, the investigator may talk to him or her about similar offenses; if the suspect is not willing to talk, investigators may use their own judgment about whether the suspect might be involved in other cases. If a suspect has been identified by a victim (as often occurs in sex crimes or robberies), previous victims may be brought in to view the suspect in a lineup.

All results of a follow up (latent) investigation are conveyed to the prosecutor in written reports. In many jurisdictions, prosecutors require investigators to consult them about the facts of a case at the time of filing. If an investigator helps solve a case, he or she may also have to testify in court.

20

Communication and Special Equipment[11]

When coordinating with either inside or street undercover agents, the surveillance agents should work out in advance a contact through which messages can be relayed by telephone. If the undercover agent becomes aware of last minute changes in the suspect's planning and a prearranged line of communication is not set up, the agent will be unable to convey this information to those on surveillance. The undercover agent might also need to identify certain suspects in the case. This, of course, must be worked out in advance with the surveillance personnel so that they can "pick up," or identify, the correct suspects. (In surveillance work, the term *pick up* should not be confused with its use as a synonym for *apprehend*. It denotes the beginning of a tail job of a particular subject at a specific location.)

Before the advent of modern radio equipment, hand signals were often the only way to accomplish the leapfrog multiple-vehicle surveillance technique. Today, nationwide companies can obtain designated wavelengths for the use of ultrahigh-frequency (UHF) radio equipment. A good radio communications consultant is the key to solving radio problems. One corporation was able to secure a radio license covering every major location in the United States within its industrial complex. This enables its corporate security department to move from locale to locale and still use its UHF radio equipment legally.

Furthermore, the use of specially equipped surveillance vans is common. Many security departments purchase stock vans from major auto manufacturers and modify them for their own surveillance use. If a surveillance van is to be disguised in some way, proper consideration should be given to the van's cover. For example, a sign on the van might advertise an industrial testing company, an engineering survey company, or a pollution study firm. If such a cover is used and signs are affixed to the van, the cover should be complete with telephone numbers for the fictitious company's answering service.

The interior of the van can be customized to meet the needs of the operation but should contain camera equipment, binoculars, a chemical toilet, and enough food and beverages to enable the agent to remain in the van for several days. A folding cot, a small table for writing reports, and other emergency equipment are required.

An innovation for surveillance vans is a type of periscope that enables the occupants of the van not only to observe their target, but also to use their camera equipment through the periscope. Lacking a periscope, the van can be rigged with blackout curtains on all windows except the one being used for observation. Special curtains of linen composition enable the occupant to view outward through a curtain, but it is virtually impossible for someone on the outside to see in.

NOTE: The remainder of this chapter was adapted from J. Kirk Barefoot, *Employee Theft Investigation*, 2d ed. (Boston: Butterworth-Heinemann, 1990).

21

Constitutional Rights[12]

The U.S. Constitution, adopted in 1789, contained few personal guarantees and some states refused to ratify it without a specific bill of rights. James Madison led the campaign to adopt the Bill of Rights, which took effect in 1791. Simply put, it is a list of rules that our government must follow to protect citizen rights.

22

Constitution, The Fourth Amendment[13]

The right of the people to be secure in their persons, houses, papers and effects, against unreasonable searches and seizures, shall not be violated, and no Warrants shall issue, but upon probable cause, supported by Oath or affirmation, and particularly describing the place to be searched, and the persons or things to be seized

The Fourth Amendment protects citizens from arbitrary police action; searches and arrests must be made with the proper legal justification. The Fourth Amendment provides guidance for the issuance of search and arrest warrants which must be based upon *probable cause*, and describe the place to be searched, and the persons or things to be seized. Probable cause is more than suspicion; it is a set of facts that would lead a reasonable person to conclude that a crime has been committed. When police believe that they have probable cause to search or arrest, they contact a magistrate who will decide whether sufficient probable cause exists to issue a warrant. Under certain circumstances, police can search and arrest without a warrant.

The landmark case of *Mapp v. Ohio*, 367 US 643, 644 (1961), illustrates the importance of Fourth Amendment protections. In this case, Cleveland police arrived at the home of Mrs. Dollree Mapp to look for evidence of a bombing, and to search for gambling paraphernalia. Mapp refused to admit the police without a warrant. Police entered the home, found pornographic material, and arrested Mapp for possession of pornography; she was convicted in an Ohio court. Because the probable cause to arrest Mapp was weak, and no search warrant was produced by the prosecution, the U.S. Supreme Court ruled that the case against Mapp violated the Fourth Amendment. This case set a famous precedent because the Court ruled that the exclusionary rule, which had applied only to the federal courts prior to this case, also applied to state courts. The *exclusionary rule* prohibits police from using illegally seized evidence at a criminal trial.

It is important to point out that the Fourth Amendment pertains to a variety of government searches, not just those conducted by police. The Fourth Amendment also regulates the searches and inspections by correctional authorities, the Occupational Safety and Health Administration, the Environmental Protection Agency, and local fire departments.

23

Constitution, The Fifth Amendment[14]

No person shall be held to answer for a capital, or otherwise infamous crime, unless on a presentment or indictment of a Grand Jury, except in cases arising in the land or naval forces, or in the Militia, when in actual service in time of War or public danger; nor shall any person be subject for the same offense to be twice put in jeopardy of life or limb; nor shall be compelled in any criminal case to be a witness against himself, nor be deprived of life, liberty, or property, without due process of law; nor shall private property be taken for public use, without just compensation.

Torture and coercion to extract confessions have existed throughout history. The Fifth Amendment provides protection, and guarantees the right to remain silent in criminal cases, civil cases, and other proceedings. In the famous case of *Miranda v. Arizona*, 384 US 436 (1966), the U.S. Supreme Court ruled that Ernesto Miranda, who confessed to Phoenix police in a kidnapping and rape case, should have been informed, prior to questioning, of his Fifth Amendment right to remain silent, part of what is called today the "Miranda warnings."

The Fifth Amendment also prohibits *double jeopardy*, which means that a person cannot be brought to trial on the same charges more than once. *Due process of law*, as stated in the Fifth Amendment, means that laws must be reasonable and applied in a fair manner while upholding individual rights.

24

Constitution, The Sixth Amendment[15]

In all criminal prosecutions, the accused shall enjoy the right to a speedy and public trial, by an impartial jury of the State and district wherein the crime shall have been committed, which district shall have been previously ascertained by law, and to be informed of the nature and cause of the accusation; to be confronted with the witnesses against him; to have compulsory process for obtaining Witnesses in his favor, and to have the Assistance of Counsel for his defense.

The Sixth Amendment emphasizes the right of defendants to a fair trial. This includes the right to a trial by an impartial jury, free from bias or prejudice against the defendant. In addition, a speedy and public trial that avoids secrecy, should expose the trial process. The Sixth Amendment covers the right to counsel, which applies to all the stages of the criminal justice process, from pretrial custody to the appellate process.

25

Constitution, The Eighth Amendment[16]

Excessive bail shall not be required, nor excessive fines imposed, nor cruel and unusual punishments inflicted.

Bail is money or property temporarily supplied by a defendant after arrest in exchange for freedom until trial. If the defendant fails to appear for trial, he/she forfeits the money or property. The Eighth Amendment does not require that bail be granted to all defendants; it requires that bail not be excessive. Because the bail system discriminates against the poor, alternatives to bail have been implemented.

The Eighth Amendment is often applied in cases brought by inmates of correctional facilities who claim that authorities subject them to "cruel and unusual punishment." Furthermore, this amendment has influenced the use of the death penalty.

26

Constitution, The Fourteenth Amendment[17]

Section 1. All persons born or naturalized in the United States, and subject to the jurisdiction thereof, are citizens of the United States and of the State wherein they reside. No State shall make or enforce any law which shall abridge the privileges or immunities of citizens of the United States; nor shall any State deprive any person of life, liberty, or property, without due process of law; nor deny to any person within its jurisdiction the equal protection of the law.

The Fourteenth Amendment has had a significant impact on criminal justice in the states. Originally, the Bill of Rights protected citizens against federal criminal proceedings only. The U.S. Supreme Court, however, has interpreted the Fourteenth Amendment's due process clause to mean that defendants charged with state crimes are entitled to rights similar to those of defendants charged with federal crimes. Thus, as we saw, for example, in the Mapp case, the Court ruled that the Fourth Amendment applies to the states through the Fourteenth Amendment.

27

Convictions: Subject/Defendant Methods to Avoid

A thief hardly ever expects to be caught at what illegal or unethical act(s) he or she may be performing or participating in. This is particularly true of the white collar criminal. This type of criminal, more so than any others, recognizes that because there are risks, they might be apprehended. Therefore, they do tend to plan a scenario of defense.

The object of your investigation will frequently engage in misdirection plans in order to establish confusion. He or she will reset the time clock and then call attention to it. They will confuse one day with another. The potential variations are limitless and as wide as their imagination will allow. Frequently, their imagination will engage "honest" witnesses and influence or control their support through manipulation and suggestion. This is why through careful questioning and investigation you must confirm or discredit the supportive data. In all instances, you should attempt to obtain statements.

If careful questioning is required of an honest witness, it is essential of a dishonest witness. Dishonest witnesses can influence their opposite number. They also can be considered for conspiracy, aiding and abetting, perjury, and taking punishment for the principal offender. Remember at all times that the defendant or perpetrator is setting the goal of introducing an element of doubt to a jury.

Defendants will frequently use the excuse of ignorance of the law or particular violation if formal charges are brought. Just as frequently if not more so, the defendant will claim that their motive was not evil. This brings into focus the state of mind of intent and motive. Lack of criminal intent is a good defense. Of course, every defendant must have been capable of understanding what he or she was doing.

Inciting the sympathy of the jury through changing appearances, using family members, and using past military service as a sympathy device are some of the methods defendants use. Other methods include discrediting the investigation, claiming illegal obtaining of evidence, claiming entrapment, and finally, the entering of a plea to a lesser charge.

28

Coordinating with the Police[18]

The question of whether and to what extent to bring the local police into a private investigation can be a thorny one. The problem arises because police patrols are bound to come into contact with stationary surveillance teams, or police officers might be dispatched in response to telephone complaints from neighbors.

When stopping surveillance agents, the police view them as suspicious persons who are loitering in the area. The officer might require the agents to get out of the vehicle and undergo a search. They might even call for an additional backup unit with the intention of taking the agents to police headquarters for further questioning. Such activity tends to attract the attention of neighbors and, of course, makes it impossible to use that location for surveillance again.

Under no circumstances should members of a surveillance team reveal to squad car personnel the target of their surveillance. It is normally sufficient for the agents to identify themselves and explain that they are on a surveillance but cannot reveal the target of the surveillance. In some small, rural communities, it might be advisable for investigators to present their driver's license and give some pretext for their presence rather than show official identification.

If the security executive decides that the local chief of police or another high-ranking police official can be trusted, he or she should try to work out an arrangement whereby members of the surveillance team would tell patrol officers, "We are on a special project with which Chief Jones is thoroughly familiar." This might not completely satisfy the patrol officer, but he or she will usually think twice before challenging the statement.

In a large police department, prior arrangements can sometimes be made so that patrol officers are informed that a surveillance car with private agents will be positioned in the area. The area so designated might not be the target of the surveillance itself but an adjoining block. Even if a certain amount of suspicion is created on the part of the local residents, it will not be apt to filter back to the suspect.

When agents are stopped by a police car for speeding, they will usually be allowed to proceed without a citation if they display proper credentials and explain to the officer that they are on a tail job involving a larceny or other crime. Again, the agents should not reveal the type of vehicle they are tailing; this information is not required. If an officer presses for additional information, it is only to satisfy personal curiosity.

If surveillance agents on a stationary stakeout of a location are approached at night by a police officer, their first act should be to turn on the car's interior light. Most police officers are extremely wary of approaching the occupants in a parked car at night. They usually do so only when they have unholstered their weapons or at least removed the safety snap from the holster. The appearance of an interior light in the automobile reduces the approaching officer's anxiety and conveys the message that the agents are legitimate and that the situation poses no undue risks.

29

Crime, Elements of

The definitions of crimes vary from state to state. However, these elements are and must be present. For example, Massachusetts General Laws Chapter 266, Section 15 includes the following definition of *burglary*: Breaking and entering of the dwelling of another in the nighttime with intent to commit a felony. It also lists these elements of the crime.

1. Breaking
2. Entry
3. Dwelling
4. Of another
5. Nighttime
6. Felonious intent

RELATED STATUTES

Not all of the statutory crimes of breaking and entering contain all elements of common law burglary.

Burglary, not being armed (F) M.G.L. c. 266, β15

Burglary, being armed or making an assault (F) M.G.L. c. 266, β14

Breaking and entering building, vehicle or ship; injury or destruction of safe or other depository of valuables (F) M.G.L. c. 266, β16

Entering in the nighttime without breaking, or in the daytime by breaking and entering, with intent to commit a felony, and causing the person lawfully therein to be put in fear (F) M.G.L. c. 266, β17

Entering dwelling house in nighttime or breaking, without putting in fear in daytime with intent to commit a felony (F) M.G.L. c. 266, β18

Breaking and entering railroad car (F) M.G.L. c. 266, β19

Making holding, using, burglarious instruments or motor vehicle master keys (F) M.G.L. c. 266, β49

30

Crime Scene Investigator's Kit Contents

- 35 mm Camera, Polaroid or VCR
- Tape measure
- Ruler with identifier
- Flashlight, additional lighting
- Tape recorder
- Maps of jurisdiction
- Clipboard, paper, pens
- New combs with envelopes
- Thermometer that measures 0 to 100 degrees (thermocouple)
- Plastic gloves
- Evidence bags
- Evidence tape
- Scotch tape
- Tools, knife, pliers, brushes
- Magnifying glass

31

Crime Scene Videotaping[19]

The availability of inexpensive portable video cameras has provided an additional means to record a crime scene. Video may provide a more complete record of a crime scene than photography by allowing one to film the entire scene. The investigator doing the taping should follow the same steps as taken when photographing a scene: Taping should begin outside the scene and then proceed to illustrate each important aspect of the crime. Attention should be given to showing each element of the *corpus delicti* of the crime. The video camera should not be turned off until the scene has been completely recorded in order to counter the defense argument that investigators altered the tape or intentionally avoided taping evidence that might be detrimental to the state's case. Generally, a videotape should be made of serious crimes of violence and crimes resulting in loss and/or damage of property of great economic value.

Some prosecutors and evidence technicians have questioned the value of videotaping a crime scene because tapes may not add a great deal to the jury's understanding of how the crime occurred and because the use of videotape may actually slow the legal proceedings against the defendant. While filming, investigators should be careful not to say anything that is not relevant to the process of gathering evidence at the scene. Videotape is subject to *discovery*, that is, the defense has the right to see and hear the tape before a trial. The defense will also insist on acquiring a transcript of the audio portion of the videotape. As with any evidence, the trial judge has the authority to excise any film that is inflammatory, and it should be expected that the defense will object to any footage that is gruesome. If, in the judgment of the prosecutor and the investigator, videotapes may aid the jury in determining the truth, it may be worthwhile to record the scene with this in mind. But it should be remembered that defense attorneys will delay a trial by requesting time to review the tape, thus making the trial more expensive and time consuming than if the tape had not been made.

32

Criminal Justice: Can Police Stop and Frisk Suspects on the Street?[20]

Experienced police officers employ what is called a sixth sense that tells them criminal activity may be afoot. Such "street smarts" cannot be taught, and come only from experience. Suppose as a police officer you observe behavior that you believe may precede a crime. What can you do? In the case of *Terry v. Ohio*, the U.S. Supreme Court provided police with legal guidelines for such incidents.

Does a *Terry stop* always result in an arrest? No, not necessarily. The suspect may be temporarily detained while being questioned and frisked, and then released. How long can a person be held for a Terry stop? In *United States v. Sharpe*, 470 US 675 (1985), the U.S. Supreme Court ruled that a 20-minute detention was reasonable, especially if the defendant causes delay by evasive action. Under the Fourth Amendment, the length of the detention should be reasonable, and depend on what police are attempting to discover, and whether they act diligently. In *United States v. Rosa Elvira Montoya de Hernandez*, 473 US 531 (1985), the Court ruled that a woman held for sixteen hours on reasonable suspicion was not unreasonable because U.S. Customs officials were attempting to verify whether she had a stomach full of balloons filled with drugs. The woman was detained for a monitored bowel movement and eighty-eight balloons of cocaine were found.

Can police handcuff a suspect during a Terry stop? In *United States v. Bautista*, 114 S.Ct. 1079 (1994), the Court ruled that the use of handcuffs during a stop and frisk does not convert the encounter into an arrest. The use of handcuffs and force must be applied in a reasonable manner with the goals of maintaining the status quo, protecting the police, and preventing escape.

Any evidence found during a Terry stop that is outside of the guidelines established by the U.S. Supreme Court will fall under the *fruit of the poisonous tree doctrine*. This doctrine labels illegally seized evidence as tainted; it cannot be used against the defendant. If as a police officer, while conducting a valid stop and frisk, you stick your hand inside of the suspect's pocket and pull out illegal drugs, is this evidence legally seized? In *Sibron v. New York*, 392 US 40 (1968), the U.S. Supreme Court ruled "no" and excluded this evidence because:

1. The suspect was not subject to a thorough search incident to an arrest;
2. The officer placed his hand inside the suspect's pockets, rather than doing a pat-down;
3. The item found was not a weapon that could create danger for the officer.

In *Minnesota v. Dickerson*, 113 S. Ct. 2130 (1993), the court ruled that an officer may seize nonthreatening contraband, such as illegal drugs, detected during a Terry pat-down if the feel of the item makes its identity "immediately apparent." However, when the officer slid and manipulated the contents of the defendant's pocket to identify the item (which was crack cocaine), the Court decided that the search went beyond what was permissible in a Terry stop.

In another case, you, a police officer on patrol, spot a group of youths who flee upon seeing your uniform. You see nothing illegal, but you know that the area is rife with heavy drug dealing, so you give chase, and see a youth throw away a small rock that looks like crack cocaine. You tackle and restrain the youth, and retrieve the substance. Later, the lab determines that it is crack cocaine. Did you act within constitutional guidelines? In the case *California v. Hodari D.*, 111 S.Ct. 1547 (1991), the U.S. Supreme Court ruled that the police chase was not a "seizure" within the meaning of the Fourth Amendment, but a "show of force" that is not unconstitutional. The seizure occurred only when the suspect was tackled. Probable cause was established when the crack was tossed and abandoned, before the tackle.

In *Delaware v. Prouse*, 440 US 648, 99 S.Ct. 1391 (1979), the U.S. Supreme Court extended the rationale of *Terry v. Ohio* to the temporary detention of motor vehicles. The propriety of conducting vehicle stops on the basis of reasonable suspicion that an occupant is or has been engaged in criminal activity including a vehicle violation, has been consistently upheld in court. The *Prouse* decision prohibited random stops, or stops for no reason. In the *Prouse* case, the officer testified that he was not answering any calls, so he decided to stop a vehicle. He smelled marijuana, saw it on the car floor, and seized it. The Court suppressed the evidence because the car stop, made with no reasonable suspicion, violated the Fourth Amendment.

Are police highway sobriety checkpoints that briefly stop motorists, unconstitutional and a violation of the Fourth and Fourteenth Amendments? In *Michigan Dept. of State Police v. Sitz*, 496 US 444, 110 S. Ct. 2481 (1990), the Court supported the State's use of a highway sobriety checkpoint as constitutional. The State's interest in preventing drunken driving outweighed the brief stop of motorists.

On the basis of reasonable suspicion that a person's luggage contains narcotics, does the Fourth Amendment allow police officers to temporarily detain the luggage to allow time for a narcotics detention dog to be brought to the scene? In *U.S. v. Place*, 462 US 696, 103 S. Ct. 2637 (1983), the Court ruled that the principles of *Terry v. Ohio* would allow police to temporarily detain luggage in a public place, up to 90 minutes, at which point detention was unreasonable and the search invalidated.

As a police officer, would you be making a Fourth Amendment "seizure" of a person if you boarded a public bus, asked passengers questions at random, asked for identification, and asked to search their luggage? The key word in this case is "asked." In *Florida v. Bostick*, 498 US 111 S. Ct. 2382 (1991), the Court upheld such police action because the requests were neither requirements nor demands. The drugs seized in this case were admissible in court even though the police had not possessed reasonable suspicion. The Court ruled that *Bostick* was not detained and could have refused the search. This case illustrates how the U.S. Supreme Court has provided the police with considerable legal authority to fight the war on illegal drugs.

33

Criminal Justice: What Are The Legal Limits Of Police Searches?[21]

The Fourth Amendment of the Constitution states: "The right of the people to be secure in their persons, houses, papers and effects, against unreasonable searches and seizures, shall not be violated, and no warrants shall issue, but upon probable cause, supported by oath and affirmation, and particularly describing the place to be searched, and the persons or things to be seized."

> Concerning a search, probable cause is a flexible, common-sense standard. It merely requires that the facts available to the officer would warrant a person of reasonable caution in the belief that certain items may be contraband [an item that is unlawful to produce or possess such as illegal drugs], or stolen property, or useful as evidence of a crime; it does not demand any showing that the belief is correct, or more likely true than false. A practical, non-technical probability that incriminating evidence is involved is all that is required."[22]

Federal and the states' constitutions support search warrants, which are the very foundation of our nation's constitutional criminal procedure. A warrant's reasonableness and validity, verified by a neutral and detached magistrate, forms the essential safeguard against government intrusion in citizens' lives.

In order to obtain a search warrant, a police officer presents facts and information that support probable cause to a magistrate or judge in the form of an application. We call this document the warrant *affidavit* and the officer who "swears out the warrant" or swears to the facts presented, the *affiant*. Police may go to a magistrate's officer, located in a courthouse or jail, or even to the home of the magistrate for a search (or arrest) warrant.

Although the Fourth Amendment makes no mention of prohibiting police use of evidence obtained in violation of this Amendment, the U.S. Supreme Court has supported the *exclusionary rule*, which is a judicial guideline used by courts to prohibit police from using illegally seized evidence at a criminal trial.

34

Criminal Justice Case Law: *Terry V. Ohio*[23]

Supreme Court of the United States, 392 US 1 (1968)

FACTS

In October of 1963 a Cleveland police detective became suspicious of three men who appeared to be "casing" a store. They repeatedly walked past the store and talked. The detective approached the three men, identified himself as a police officer, asked for their names, patted down the outside of their clothing, and found .38 caliber revolvers on two of the men. Both men were charged with carrying concealed weapons.

QUESTION TO THE COURT

Are a citizen's Fourth Amendment rights against unreasonable search and seizure violated when police stop and frisk the subject, if police have reasonable suspicion to believe that the subject is armed and dangerous? *Reasonable suspicion* is grounds to suspect that a person has committed, is committing, or is about to commit a crime; it is less than probable cause.

DECISION

The U.S. Supreme Court provided six guidelines for a stop and frisk: (1) reasonable suspicion by police that criminal activity is afoot; (2) reasonable suspicion that the subject may be armed and dangerous; (3) police must identify themselves; (4) police make a reasonable inquiry; (5) nothing in the initial stages of the confrontation dispels police officer's fear; and (6) police conducted a limited search of outer clothing to discover weapons.

35

Criminal Justice Case Law: *Mapp v. Ohio*[24]

Supreme Court of the United States 367 US 643, 644 (1961).

FACTS

This famous case began in May of 1957 when Cleveland police arrived at the residence of Mrs. Dollree Mapp to search for a suspect in a recent bombing, and to search for gambling paraphernalia. Mapp called her attorney and refused to admit the police without a search warrant. When additional officers arrived, police forced their way into the home. Mapp's attorney arrived, but police blocked his entrance and refused to let him see his client. As police entered, Mapp demanded to see the search warrant and an officer held up a paper. The paper was grabbed by Mapp and stuffed in her bra. The police forcibly removed the paper and handcuffed Mapp. While conducting a though search, the police found a trunk in the basement containing pornographic literature. Neither the bombing suspect nor gambling paraphernalia were found. Mapp was arrested for possession of pornography and convicted in an Ohio court. During the trial, no search warrant was produced by the prosecution.

When the case reached the U.S. Supreme Court, it faced the question of the legality of the arrest, search, and seizure. Specifically, the probable cause to arrest Mapp was weak, and the existence of a search warrant was questionable.

QUESTION TO THE COURT

Does the exclusionary rule apply to the states?

DECISION

Yes. Evidence obtained in violation of the Fourth Amendment must be excluded from state as well as federal trials.

36

Criminal Justice Case Law: *Mapp v. Ohio* Analysis and Impact[25]

The central issue of the *Mapp* case was the exclusionary rule and its applicability to the states. In 1914, the U.S. Supreme Court, in *Weeks v. U.S.*, 232 US 383, prohibited federal agents from using illegally seized evidence in federal courts. This solidified Fourth Amendment prohibitions against unreasonable search and seizure on the federal level but it did not include state actions. The *Weeks* decision ruled in the *silver platter doctrine* whereby federal prosecutors used illegally seized evidence provided by state and local police who obtained the evidence without federal participation. This practice ended with *Elkins v. U.S.*, 364 US 206 (1960), one year before Mapp.

When the Mapp decision was handed down, prosecutors raised an uproar. They complained that they themselves were being "handcuffed," deprived of their authority to search and gather evidence. They claimed that criminals would go free and crime would rise. Contrary to these claims, the Mapp decision enhanced police professionalism by forcing them to use Fourth Amendment law rather than bullying tactics. Police learned to work "smarter" while upholding constitutional rights.

The Mapp decision came under attack from several quarters—police, citizens, Congress, and even the Court itself. The exclusionary rule generated tremendous controversy and resulted in decisions that did not overturn Mapp, but provided exceptions to the rule:

- *Purged taint exception:* A voluntary act by the defendant removes the taint of earlier illegal police conduct. For example, if the defendant makes a voluntary statement, it is unaffected by an earlier illegal arrest. *Wong Sun v. United States,* 371 US 471 (1963).
- *Independent untainted source exception:* Police obtain evidence that is independent of the illegally obtained evidence. For example, an in court identification of the defendant is admissible even if the defendant's original arrest was illegal. *United States v. Crews,* 445 US 463 (1980).
- *Good faith exception:* Evidence gathered by police acting in good faith in accordance with a search warrant issued by a neutral and detached magistrate is admissible, even though the warrant is found to be defective. For example, police, in good faith, execute a search warrant (issued by a magistrate) that fails to establish probable cause. *United States v. Leon,* 468 US 897 (1984).
- *Inevitable discovery exception:* The police would have discovered evidence even though the confession was obtained illegally. See *Nix v. Williams,* 467 US 431 (1984).

37

Criminal Law in the United States Today[26]

In the United States, the five major sources of criminal law are (1) common law, (2) statutes passed by Congress and state legislatures; (3) case law, (4) administrative law, and (5) federal and state constitutions. Following the American Revolution, Americans acknowledged the worth of the English system of common law, but questioned its clarity or diffusion, scattered as it was throughout hundreds of common law case books, and the power it gave judges. A movement began to codify the criminal law, first at the federal level and later at the state level.[27]

Federal and state constitutions, with court rulings creating precedents, have provided the power for legislative bodies to enact criminal and civil statutes. Derived from common law, *statutes* are precise laws defining and prohibiting crimes. The U.S. Congress enacts federal statutes and state legislatures enact state statutes. On the local level, city and county councils enact ordinances. All these statutes and ordinances are compiled into codes. Thus, we have the U.S. Code (USC), state codes, and local codes. State and local codes (retaining a mixture of statutory and common law) are far from uniform and vary among jurisdictions; what may be illegal in one jurisdiction may be legal in another.

Criminal law is classified as substantive law and procedural law. *Substantive law* defines criminal offenses such as murder or robbery, and specifies corresponding fines and punishment. Federal and state governments differ in the way they define and punish offenses. Criminal codes reflect the beliefs and values of our society and change over time. *Procedural law* covers the formal rules for enforcing substantive law, and the steps required to process a criminal case; the laws of arrest, search and seizure, the right to counsel, jury selection, and the rules of evidence.

Court decisions interpret constitutional law, render case decisions, and clarify the wording of legislation and statutes. As distinguished from statutes and constitutions, which are written in the abstract, *case law* establishes judicial precedent by the judicial reasoning and rulings that resolve unique disputes. Case law concerns concrete facts.[28] When subsequent cases are decided upon precedent, it is referred to as the principle of stare decisis (as we saw with common law). This principle facilities fairness and predictability in the legal system.

Administrative law is the legal basis awarded by legislatures and courts to administrative agencies that allows them to regulate parts of our society. On the federal level (states have similar agencies), for example, the Environmental Protection Agency (EPA) protects the environment and the Occupational Safety and Health Administration (OSHA) ensures a safe workplace. Legislators, lacking the technical expertise, have delegated power to these agencies which hold the full force of law to make rules, conduct investigations, enforce rules, and conduct hearings. Although it may be argued that administrative agencies, for good or ill, are independent of legislatures and less susceptible to direct political control, these agencies are controlled by funding, their charters can be modified, and they can be dissolved.[29]

The U.S. Constitution contains basic principles regarding powers of the federal government, the powers reserved to the states, and the rights of citizens as specified in the Bill of Rights. The courts interpret the Constitution and render decisions on constitutional issues, such as whether a (federal or state) law violates the Constitution by being too vague or too broad. Constitutions support state governments as well. A state's constitution, although subordinate to the U.S. Constitution, is the supreme law within that state and superior to any local government constitution or charter.

38

Criminal Law's Purposes: Theory versus Reality[30]

Criminal law exists to formally identify conduct that harms individuals and the community, and to enable the state to formally control and punish those who commit crime. Sociologists call the rules of society *norms*, and refer to folkways and mores. *Folkways*, like talking loudly in public, are morally insignificant norms and unenforced. *Mores* are serious, strictly enforced norms such as the more against murder. Laws are formal expressions of norms.[31]

Theoretically, criminal law proposes to deter potential offenders by threatening concrete punishment. In reality, research on the outcome of felony arrests shows that only 32 percent are sentenced to prison.[32] For every 1,000 young persons in contact with police, one percent will serve a sentence in a state program.[33]

As criminologist Joseph F. Sheley points out, research into whether *deterrence*, threatened or actual punishment, effectively prevents crime has produced weak and ambiguous results.[34] Throughout history, when the punishment for crime was made more severe, this strategy did not deter crime. In England during the early 1800s, about 233 crimes were punishable by death.[35] Yet, while pickpockets were being hung, more pickpockets were working the crowd.[36] More recently, in the 1970s in New York State, which claimed to have the nation's toughest drug law, characterized by mandatory and long prison terms, neither drug usage nor drug related crime declined.[37]

Since criminal law specifies the punishment for an offense, theoretically, this should ensure uniform punishment for the same crime. Research shows, however, not only wide variations in sentencing, but that race influences variable sentencing.

39

Cutting and Stabbing Investigations: 5 Things You Should Know

1. This is defined as cutting and stabbing with edged and pointed instruments. Three types of wounds are caused: cut, stab and chop.
2. Wound characteristics:
   Type of instrument or weapon
   Size of weapon
   Direction of injury
   Position of victim
   Time of injury (inflammatory response)
   Was force used?
3. Questions: Was it homicidal? Was it suicidal? Was it accidental?
4. Cut or incised wound characteristics:
   Clean edges
   Minimum bruising
   No bridging of skin

Longer than deep
Any overlaying hair would be cut
Bleeds freely
Instrument seldom indicated by wound
Little trace evidence
Cannot determine: Weapon length, weapon size, single or double edge, amount of force

5. Stab wound characteristics:
Result of pointed or sharp object being forced inwards
Deeper than wide
Presents danger to vital structures
Often bleeds internally with little or no external blood
May indicate type of weapon used
Usually no abrasion to edge
May break off in wound and give a match of the weapon
May give *minimum* and *maximums* of weapon
Knife hilt may bruise skin and leave identifiable mark
May *perforate* organ as well as *penetrate* body

40

Description Identification

People normally see only your face and hands; the other 90 percent they see is clothing. Obviously, you must have as complete a description as possible if it is to successfully identify someone.

The obvious:

name	approximate height	moustache
aliases	approximate age	chin
address	approximate weight	face
sex	build	neck
race	eyes	shoulders
hair	complexion	hands
nose	lips	posture
walk	speech/voice tone	dress
	tatoos	visible scars/marks

The not so obvious:

citizenship	teeth
national origin	ears
body marks	stomach
occupation	body scars
marital status	habits
head	diseases
forehead	relatives
eyebrows	pastimes
associates	

OBJECTS

When describing a manufactured object, identify it by name. State the date made, model or type, size, weight, shape and color. Ascertain what material or combination of materials it is made of. It is important to state the intended use of the object. It is equally as important to state what it was actually used for it different. Describe the condition as to age, use, and wear. List marks such as serial numbers and any other numbers noted, letters, words, monograms, or any insignia. If any marks or defects or damages are visible, they must be listed. Be sure to list where the object was found and photograph and/or sketch it.

SKETCHES

The purpose of a sketch is to supplement photographs, digital photographs, and written or oral statements. Usually there are only three kinds of sketches: of general location, specific scene(s), and details of a scene. The essential elements in sketching are: you must have a specific subject in mind; indicate the compass points; indicate the scale to which the drawing is made; and date the sketch. Of course, you would want to show all the large objects at the scene and all the parts that have a bearing on your investigation. When sketching a room, show the floor plan and all objects that are attached to the floor, entrances and exits, all four walls, objects and equipment present, and anything that is pertinent to your investigation.

41

Diversion: Grey Goods Investigation and Prevention

Any manufacturer would be wise to screen its product sales and distribution. The acts of diversion that can plague a company are frequently nothing more than white collar crime. Product diversion erodes markets, devalues brand names, destroys a quality reputation or image, negatively impacts on sales, and can create potential liabilities. Certainly, these concerns individually would suggest that customer, distributor, and client screening are a must.

Traditional reliance upon registering and/or obtaining a trademark is not sufficient. While the intent of a trademark is to protect the brand name, it is not adequate to deter diversion and grey market operators. Trade names are protected on a country-by-country basis. While each country protects trademarks in accordance with its own business practices, they are not necessarily registered.

Investigations and prevention efforts should follow the following categories:

- Unfair competition
- Infringement
- Misrepresentation and fraud
- Breach of contract
- Conspiracy to defraud
- Deceptive and unfair business practices
- Dilution of trademark integrity

The U.S. laws that apply may include those listed below, either individually or in combination:

- 18 US Code 1964
- 28 US Code 1331 and 1332
- 18 US Code 1341—Mail Fraud
- 18 US Code 1343—Wire Fraud
- 18 US Code 2314—Transportation
- 15 US Code 1114—Federal Trademark Infringement
- 15 US Code 1125—False Designation of Origin and False Description or Representation to Retailers

Delivery conditions for goods must include that the product is being sold on condition and understanding that it shall be offered for sale in specifically agreed upon locations. The buyer warrants that the product will be delivered to the agreed upon location and remain offered for sale or use at that location. The buyer should furnish a signed bill of lading and copy of the export declaration if originating in the United States. Other appropriate documents used in international logistical transactions may also be required.

42

Protocols for Grey Goods Control Diversion

Listed below are ten specific recommendations or protocols which may be implemented by companies for use in transshipment control:

1. All sales and operating employees shall not engage in or support any activities associated with or in support of distribution and sales of its products which results in diversion or transshipments to unauthorized dealers, retailers, or secondary marketers. This shall also apply to suppliers, vendors, or contract employees.
2. Pricing, both domestic and international, should be in the currency of the origin country and uniform in order to reduce or eliminate exchange rate arbitrage.
3. Applications for distributors, retailers, and transporters shall have a due diligence review and business relationship background conducted prior to any agreements for shipments or backgrounds.
4. A task group should be formed by each manufacturer for the purpose of control of product integrity. Membership should consist of representatives of all concerned departments including financial, legal, sales, security, and operations.
5. There should be no approval for shipments or sales disproportionate to realistic abilities of the consignees to sell at retail or distribute.
6. There should be periodic reviews and audits conducted over all domestic and international distributors and retailers. Also included in this process should be all transportation, warehouses, and duty free activities.

7. An agreed upon termination policy should be in place and binding for all customers, clients, and distributors that are proven to be engaged in diversion or transhipment activities.
8. Absolutely no "drop" shipments should be allowed.
9. All large volume and "international" sales should have special markings and packaging.
10. Customers, clients, distributors, retailers, and any other means of product sale shall be given a specific identification, associated only with the individual recipient of the identification.

43

Documentary Evidence

It is obvious that when it comes to documentary evidence, there is much more immediately available to public enforcement through laws of arrest and seizure legally supported by the courts and the specific laws and/or regulations at issue. A witness, regardless of whether public or private enforcement is the instrument requesting books and records, has a legal right to refuse to produce these items if they would tend to incriminate him or her. A corporate officer must produce the corporation's books and records even if they may incriminate him or her and/or the corporation. However, he or she cannot be compelled to testify about the corporation's business if that testimony would tend to incriminate them. Interestingly, if their testimony would not incriminate them but would incriminate the corporation, he or she has no right to refuse to testify.

There are two types of sworn statements that fall in the documentary evidence category: affidavits and depositions. An *affidavit* is a sworn statement given by a witness or a defendant. You take the affidavit generally to make a record of what the person will testify to in court, if necessary. Some civil cases are tried by affidavits only and in this case the affidavits are accepted as evidence. In a criminal case this is not the case as the defendant, under the Sixth Amendment to the U.S. Constitution, has the right to be confronted with the witnesses against them.

Depositions are sworn statements usually requested by judicial order, in which both sides are or have the option to be present so that they may question the person. This is most generally reserved for civil cases and is very rare in criminal cases.

When dealing with documentation evidence, the original document(s) is the best evidence and must be produced. There are exceptions to this when the original(s) is not available either through being lost, destroyed, or simply beyond the reach of the court process. This is the case when an original document(s) is in the hands of an accused because he or she is not compelled to comply with, or produce, the document(s) requested.

When legal documentary evidence is located in many locations and in many different books, ledgers, and computers, an auditor can summarize them and then use the summaries as evidence. He or she would be testifying as an expert witness. Of course, the opposite party must be given the opportunity to examine the books, ledgers, and computers, too.

44

Drug And Alcohol Testing Equipment[38]

The use or possession of alcohol and illegal or controlled substances by students is not unfamiliar to school administrators and security and law enforcement personnel. Along with traditional education and drug-resistance programs in the schools and the community, proactive prevention and deterrence measures must be in place and publicized to all students.

Recent court decisions have ruled in favor of school districts that conduct the random drug testing of student athletes, but the testing of other students is still conditioned on reasonable suspicion by school administrators. Should administrators suspect a student to be under the influence of alcohol or drugs, they should have available in the school a "breathalyzer" and presumptive drug testing kits. These tests can consist of a simple chemical test which changes color in the presence of alcohol or specific suspect drugs.

Another effective deterrence measure is to use drug detection dogs to randomly inspect lockers and cars. Dogs can also be used to inspect student belongings. In this case, as an example, students are asked to leave their belongings (book bags, coats, purses, etc.) at their desks and to leave the classroom as a class with the teacher before the dog and handler enter the room. Drug detection dogs and their handlers are usually available from local law enforcement agencies and can usually be requested with advanced planning and scheduling. Explosive detection dogs (trained to detect traces of gun powder and other explosives) may also be available from local or state law enforcement agencies to seek out guns, bullets, and explosive related material. Some school districts have their own drug detection dog and handler as part of the school security/police department.

45

Electronic Surveillance and Wiretapping[39]

Electronic surveillance is the use of electronic devices to covertly listen to conversations, while wiretapping is the covert interception of telephone communications. Eavesdropping and wiretapping can be both legal and illegal. When legal, it is carried out by authority of a warrant issued in accord with the law. The extent of such legal activity is measurable (at least theoretically) in the number of warrants issued. Illegal eavesdropping and wiretapping, on the other hand, defy measurement because they are carried out secretively.

Given the stakes in modern business dealings and the opportunities to easily steal sensitive business information, we can comfortably conclude, without fear of badly missing the mark, that the theft of business information by these illegal means is pervasive.

SURVEILLANCE EQUIPMENT AND TECHNIQUES

Surveillance equipment is easy to obtain. An electronically inclined person can simply buy from an electronics wholesaler or retailer the parts and instructions for making a workable bug. Prebuilt models are available by mail with no strings attached, and some retailers sell them across the counter after taking nothing more than a signed statement from the purchaser that the equipment will not be used in violation of the law.

Mall and neighborhood electronics stores sell inexpensive wireless FM microphones and transmitters that can be used for covert listening purposes. These devices can pick up conversations and send them across considerable distances to a recording unit and waiting eavesdroppers. They are sometimes advertised as innocent pieces of equipment that can be useful to mothers in monitoring the activities of their children in other parts of the house.

Miniaturization has greatly aided spying. With advances in microchip technology, transmitters can be so small as to be enmeshed in wallpaper, inserted under a stamp, or placed on the head of a nail. Transmitters are capable of being operated by solar power or local radio broadcast. Bugging systems even enable the interception and decoding of typewriter and duplicating machine transmissions.

Bugging techniques vary. Information from a microphone can be transmitted via a wire run or a radio transmitter. Bugs can be concealed in a variety of objects or carried on a person and remotely turned on and off by radio signals. A device known as a carrier current transmitter can be placed in a wall plug, light switch, or similar electrical receptacle. It obtains power from the AC wire to which it is attached. Devices are difficult to detect by visual inspection when they are cleverly concealed and difficult to detect by electronic analysis when they are turned off.

Telephone lines are especially vulnerable to tapping. Telephone lines are accessible in such great numbers and in so many places that taps are easy to install and difficult to find. A tap can be direct or wireless. With a direct tap, a pair of wires is spliced to the telephone line and then connected to a tape recorder concealed someplace not too far away. The direct tap can only be detected by a check of the entire line. With the wireless tap, an FM transmitter is connected to the line, and the transmitter sends the intercepted conversation to a receiver and tape recorder. Wireless taps (and room bugs) are spotted by using special equipment. For the spy, the wireless tap is safer than the direct tap because investigators can follow the wires to the spy's hiding place.

Another technique transforms the telephone into a listening device whether it is in use or not. A technique known as the hookswitch bypass causes the hookswitch to not disconnect when the receiver is replaced. Although the telephone is disconnected, the telephone's microphone is still active. The effect is to transform the telephone into a listening bug. This technique can be detected by hanging up the telephone, tapping into the telephone line, making noise near the telephone, and listening for the noise on the telephone tap.

The spy may use a dual system in which two bugs are placed: the first to be found and the second so well concealed that it may escape detection. Discovery of the first bug is to lull management into false complacency.

46

Employee Applications

We recently were investigating an employee's job application and found the following:

1. It was incomplete.
2. He lied about his high school and college courses.
3. The previous job reference had the wrong address.
4. One of his personal references was nonexistent.

Why do we have job applications? There are several reasons:

1. To determine the accuracy of an applicant by verifying the completeness of the application
2. To determine if an applicant is a proper candidate for employment
3. To determine if there are gaps in employment
4. To determine omissions of fact or false statements
5. To determine previous employment and proper references

In the event of a bad application, follow the golden rule—"Don't hire the individual!" A problem application will turn out to be a problem employee. Remember:

1. A completed application has adequate information.
2. Background investigations must be completed before employment.
3. References, personally checked, as well as a visit with neighbors, should be considered.

Access to the applicant's criminal history record is a key issue in pre-employment screening. It has become a supplemental source in the hiring process.

47

Entrapment[40]

Entrapment is the act of officers or agents of the government in inducing persons to commit crimes not previously contemplated by them for the purpose of instituting criminal prosecutions. This occurs when the criminal design originates with a government official and is implanted in the mind of an innocent person who does not otherwise have the predisposition to commit the offense charged. The idea of committing the crime originates with law enforcement officers or their agents who artificially propagate the inception of the crime. A law enforcement agent includes any person who acts in concert, in accordance, or in cooperation with the law enforcement official. A private citizen who does this becomes an extension of the law enforcement official's arm. Security managers should be aware of the cooperative activities of their staffs with law enforcement so as to prevent opening this affirmative defense to the potential defendant. Entrapment does not result from an act of inducement by a private citizen.

48

Ethical Issues for Investigative Personnel[41]

Investigators are often caught on the horns of ethical dilemmas whether they are publicly or privately employed. Some of these are:

- Role/duty confusion by private and security investigators. The question of primary loyalty to clients, employers and courts comes into play.

- Violations of privacy.
- Unauthorized disclosure of confidential information.
- The use of deception as an investigative technique. Sometimes innocent persons are lied to. Emotions may also be played with in order to gain information.
- The use of personal intimacy (friendship or romance) to gather information.
- Developing informants is sometimes done through personal relationships with others. Using people to acquire information is a common tactic that some persons may find repugnant.
- Pressure to obtain results in some cases. This includes those that are highly publicized as well as those where there is indignation on the part of managers who want results. Undercover investigators are often pressured to obtain results as this type of investigation usually takes a lot of time and is very expensive.
- The temptation to entrap suspects. Many are "scumbags" and deserve to be punished in the mind of the investigator. Entrapment or perjury is easily rationalized when used against repulsive criminals; especially when it may appear (options may not be explored) that there are no legally acceptable methods of prosecuting them.
- Coercion is used to get statements and confessions. This probably doesn't involve physical threats but instead relies on psychological pressure. A common tactic is to have a suspect "roll over" on his or her associates in exchange for dropping charges.
- Exaggeration and falsification of expenses where financial controls are lax and reimbursement of personal funds is limited. If investigators feel they are underpaid—and they may well be—and are asked to work extensive amounts of time, travel a lot, and spend their own money, this is easy to rationalize. In private investigations it may also be the case that the client is not being billed at an appropriate rate: the padding of expenses is done to adjust the billing.
- Avoidance of responsibility by managers of undercover operations. In many cases, as long as results are being obtained, management is loathe to inquire about the psychological and emotional well-being of the agent. Changes in personality and behavior that indicate problems are ignored. Questionable investigative practices that the operative engages in are consciously overlooked or minimized.
- Abuse of informants may occur in vice investigations. Those involved with criminal activity or those who are on the fringes of illicit behavior are often "used and abused." Investigators may coerce them, reward them with illegal materials (drugs, contraband), or allow them to participate in minor forms of criminality (prostitution, small time drug dealing, petty amounts of poaching, etc.). Unfortunately, in some cases the "little fish" used to catch the "big fish" are not always "little fish" in the criminal world. Some become major criminals who act with some degree of impunity derived from their cooperation with investigators. In other cases, informants are coerced into providing information, introductions, and so forth at great risk to themselves, only to be cast aside when the investigation is completed.

COUNCIL OF INTERNATIONAL INVESTIGATORS CODE OF ETHICS

1. To conduct myself in my profession with honesty, sincerity, integrity, fidelity, morality and good conscience in all my dealings with my clients.
2. To preserve forever my Clients' confidences under any and all circumstances except where the Clients' interest is contrary to criminal law.
3. To conduct all my investigations within the bounds of legality, morality and professional ethics.
4. To refuse to employ the methods of wiretapping in any form in those countries where it is unlawful.
5. To retain in the strictest confidence every facet of my Clients' interest from inquiries by third parties especially in matters involving national notoriety or publicity.
6. To cooperative with all recognized and responsible law enforcement and governmental agencies in matters within the realm of their jurisdiction.
7. To counsel my Client against any illegal or unethical course of action.
8. To explain to the full satisfaction of my Client all fees and charges in his case and to render a factual report.
9. To retain my own professional reputation and that of my fellow investigators and professional associates.
10. To ensure that all my employees adhere to this Code of Ethics.

49

Evidence Collection and Processing[42]

Studies show that many crime scenes contain physical evidence linking a suspect with the crime. To collect this evidence (primarily fingerprints), many departments use a trained evidence technician whose sole task is to process crime scenes. Technicians may be dispatched at the time of the crime report, or they may be sent out following the initial report if the responding patrol officer feels that usable evidence might be found. Their job is to examine the crime scene, lift any latent fingerprints, and submit a report of their results to the responsible unit.

50

Evidence Gathering and Transporting

However you elect to identify evidence you must mark or tag as well as transport it for safekeeping. In order for the collection of evidence to be acceptable in the various courts, it must conform to the rules of evidence. Whatever method is selected—either numbering, lettering, or some other combination thereof—a log must be kept. Listed below are some suggested or recommended methods of transporting evidence:

- Documentation disks and tapes are to be placed in cellophane bags without folds. Mark the exterior of the bag with details of place, time, date, conditions and any other pertinent data.
- Hairs, fibers, soil, fingernails, and residue are to be first placed in bond paper and than cellophane bags with appropriate marks.
- Garments with blood or other liquids should be first allowed to dry naturally and then placed within individual cellophane bags and marked.
- Liquids, oils, and grease are to be left in containers within which they were found. If they are not in a container, place them in specimens or clean glass bottles.
- Glass or glasslike substances are to be lain on strips of cardboard and layers built up. If available, place on clay on a flat surface or on a clay bed. Twist cap the specimens with paper. Never allow the glass to touch or clang together.
- Knives or scissors should be lain flat on a surface that can be penetrated by holds to tie the object in question down.
- Weapons should be placed in a box. A gun should be secured with a trigger lock and the box locked and secured.
- Lead slugs or casings should be placed in paper without touching and twisted like salt water taffy.
- Paint, paint chips, or flecks are to be collected along with the sample of the paint to be matched (known as the *control*) marked accordingly, and placed in a cellophane bag.
- Food/beverage substances are to be kept in the containers in which they are found.
- Substances/liquids that may evaporate quickly must be tightly sealed.

When tagging evidence, there are seven basic items to be noted. These are:

1. The crime(s)
2. Name and address of the victim or the accused
3. Date of the crime
4. Place of the crime
5. Brief description of the article, where it was found, and what part in relation to the crime
6. Who you represent or are affiliated with
7. Your name

51

Examination Types[43]

DNA EXAMINATIONS

Deoxyribonucleic acid (DNA) is analyzed in body fluids and body fluid stains recovered from physical evidence in violent crimes. DNA analysis is conducted utilizing the restriction fragment length polymorphism (RFLP) method or other appropriate DNA methods. Evidence consists of known liquid and dried blood samples, portions of rape kit swabs, and extracts and body fluid stained cuttings from homicide, sexual assault, and serious aggravated assault cases.

The results of DNA analysis on a questioned body fluid stain are compared visually and by computer image analysis to the results of DNA analysis on known blood samples as a means of potentially identifying or excluding an individual as the source of a questioned stain. As such, this technique, similar to fingerprinting, is capable of directly associating a victim of a violent crime with the subject or the subject with the crime scene. The implementation of this technique in the laboratory represents a significant advance in forensic serology.

CHEMICALS

Toxicological Examinations

A toxicological examination looks for the presence of drugs and/or poisons in biological tissues and fluids. The toxicological findings show whether the victim of a crime died or became ill as the result of drug or poison ingestion, or whether the involved persons were under the influence of drugs at the time of the matter under investigation.

Because of the large number of potentially toxic substances, it is necessary (unless a specific toxic agent is implicated prior to examination) to screen biological samples for classes of poisons. Examples of these classes and the drugs and chemicals that may be found within these classes are as follows:

- Volatile compounds, such as ethanol, carbon monoxide and chloroform
- Heavy metals, such as arsenic, mercury, thallium and lead
- Inorganic ions, such as cyanide, azide, chloride, and bromide
- Nonvolatile organize compounds, such as most drugs of abuse and other pharmaceuticals, as well as pesticides and herbicides

Drug and Pharmaceutical Examinations

The forensic laboratory will determine if materials seized as suspected drugs do in fact contain controlled substances. In addition, the laboratory can examine a wide variety of items, such as boats, aircraft, automobiles, clothing, luggage, and money, for the presence of trace quantities of cocaine, heroin, phencyclidine (PCP), and so forth. A pharmaceutical examination will identify products for the purpose of matching recovered products with stolen products, or for proving that pharmaceuticals were switched.

Arson Examinations

The gas chromatography technique is used to determine the presence of accelerants or other substances introduced to a fire scene to facilitate destruction. Debris collected from the scene of a suspected arson can be analyzed to learn if a distillate was used to accelerate the fire and if so, testing can classify the distillate by product, such as gasoline, fuel oil, or paint solvent. Debris most suitable for analysis will be absorbent in nature, such as padded furniture, carpeting, plasterboard and flooring.

General Chemical Examinations

Qualitative and quantitative analyses can be made of miscellaneous chemical evidence. Quality analysis is helpful in cases involving theft or contamination of chemical products, malicious destruction, and assault. Analysis of writing inks can match questioned documents with known ink specimens obtained from typewriter ribbons and stamp pads. In consumer product tampering cases, analysis can determine the presence and nature of contaminants, adulterants, and alterations to containers. Chemical examinations can be useful in evaluating tear gas and dyes in bank robber packers, constituents determination in patent fraud cases, and flash and water soluble paper in gambling and spy cases.

52

Examinations: The Functions of DNA Testing[44]

DNA testing provides a basis for positive identification, but is it not expected to become a suitable technology for validating identification in security settings. DNA analysis would be inappropriate in situations where a nearly immediate determination must be made as to whether a person seeking entry to a particular area, or seeking to conduct a particular transaction is, in fact, authorized to do so. The chemical analysis required to make a DNA comparison takes weeks, not minutes. DNA testing is increasingly used to determine paternity and, in forensic settings, it has been most prolifically and successful used to identify or exonerate a suspect.

PATERNITY DETERMINATIONS

In determining paternity, DNA has proven to be extraordinarily useful. Each chromosome contains nucleotides identical to those of each part, as well as the nucleotides that distinguish the individuality of the person. If samples from the child and from one of the parents are available, the nucleotides of the child that are different from the known parent's DNA must have come from the unknown parent's DNA. If a sample from the suspected, but unknown, parent supplies all the "missing" nucleotides without any superfluous nucleotides, one can conclude that the suspect individual is, in fact, the other parent.

IDENTIFICATION OF SUSPECTS

The forensic promise of DNA typing is substantial. Samples of human skin, hair follicles, blood, semen, or saliva containing cells or other tissues found on a crime victim or at a crime scene can be examined to identify the DNA pattern. That pattern can be compared with DNA from a suspect to make a "positive identification," or to exonerate a suspect. DNA examination techniques sometimes permit the use of extraordinarily small samples of human tissues or fluids, such as a few hairs or a single spot of blood. Moreover, DNA is durable and is relatively resistant to adverse environmental conditions such as heat or moisture. DNA degrades slowly in a decomposing body, lasting sometimes for years and allowing samples to be analyzed for some time after the death of an individual. Although some experts debate the percentage of usable tissue and fluid samples that are retrieved from all crime scenes, DNA analysis will have the greatest effect on violent crime cases such as murder and rape, where hair, blood, semen, or tissue evidence is frequently found.

53

Factors and Theories in Criminality[45]

The relationship between economic factors and criminality is extremely complex. Poverty can bring about crime, but its social conditions may be more important than the economic circumstances in producing crime. To the radical or critical criminologist, criminality is one of the consequences of the class struggle in a capitalist society. Criminal law and the criminal justice system are viewed as tools used by the power elite to maintain the status quo and exclude the poor and disenfranchised from sharing power and wealth.

The nature versus nurture issue has never entirely disappeared from criminology theories since the time of Lombroso. But genetic studies of criminality have progressed considerably since the turn of the twentieth century, when investigators traced the genealogies of families distinguished by unusually high percentages of criminals, lunatics, and mental defectives.

The strongest evidence for a view of inherited criminality has come from the studies of chromosomes, with a particular abnormality being found disproportionately among male criminals. Men with the XYY combination of chromosomes (XY being normal) have a ten to twenty time greater tendency to break the law than do genetically normal men.

Research on the study of identical and fraternal twins also suggests some evidence of linkage between genetics and criminality. The results of a dozen studies in Europe, Asia, and the United States suggest that identical as contrasted with fraternal twins with a criminal record are twice as likely to have a co-twin with a record. The differential resemblance of identical and fraternal twins is generally considered to be strong, though not be itself conclusive.

In a study of the criminal connections of more than 4,000 adopted Danish boys, it was determined that they were more dependent on their biological than their adoptive parents' criminality. The more serious an offender a biological parent was, the greater the risk of criminality for his or her child, particularly for property crimes. Adopted boys who had a chronically criminal biological parent (three or more convictions) were three times more likely to become criminal than those whose biological parents were not criminal.

In the study of the relationship between IQ and criminality, many studies have shown that the offender population has an average IQ of about 91–93, compared with an average IQ of 100 for the population at large. In general, the most common offenses, impulsive violent crimes and opportunistic property crimes, are most often committed by people in the low normal and borderline retarded range.

Psychiatrists have interpreted crime as a syndrome or category of mental illness. Psychologists, on the other hand, have tended to view criminality as behavior that is acquired in the same way as other patterns of learned behavior—that is, through reinforcement. The psychiatric approach has fostered two lines of inquiry: (1) the search for a "criminal personality," and (2) the assessment of psychiatric disorders among criminals. Both of these areas of research have failed to provide results that confirm the theories on which they are based. Neither clinical observations nor psychological tests have identified any cluster of psychological traits distinctive to the criminal. With the exception of alcoholism, drug addiction, and sociopathy or psychopathy—terms often defined with reference to the criminal behavior they are supposed to explain—psychiatric disorders appear to occur with about the same frequency in both criminal and noncriminal populations.

Social learning theory asserts that people learn both deviant behavior and the definitions that go along with them. The learning can be direct, as through conditioning, or indirect, as through imitation and modeling. Learned deviance can then be strengthened by reinforcement or weakened by punishment. Its continued maintenance depends not only on its own reinforcement but also on the quality of the reinforcement given for alternative behavior. If the definitions of deviant behavior are reinforcing and if alternative behaviors are not reinforced as strongly, then the individual is likely to engage in deviant behaviors (F. P. Williams, III and M. D. McShane. *Criminological Theories.* Englewood Cliffs, NJ: Prentice-Hall, 1988).

Sociological theories of criminality are directed toward finding answers to questions about collective rather than individual criminal behavior. There are two approaches to the exploration and interpretation of social factors in crime causation. The structural approach looks at the influence of social patterns of power or institutions on criminality. The subcultural approach emphasizes the role of conflict between the norms of the larger society and those characteristics of lower-class or ethnic subcultures. The latter approach maintains that when the norms of the subculture impose standards of conduct different from those prescribed by the larger culture, the resulting normative conflict can become the major source of criminal behavior.

Sociopsychological theories of criminality examine the processes by which people become delinquents or criminals and the differential response factors that help explain why some people who are exposed to adverse environmental conditions engage in crime and delinquency while others do not. Sutherland's differential association theory suggests that crime is learned principally in primary groups. Reckless's containment theory attempts to consider both social and cultural factors (outer containment) and individual factors (inner containment) and the way these factors interact to produce crime and delinquency. Finally, the labeling perspective focuses on societal reactions to deviant behavior. The imposition of a deviant label may result in increasing, rather than decreasing, tendencies to engage in criminal behavior. According to this approach, formal treatment of deviant behavior may do more harm than good.

54

Family Violence and Violence Against Women: 17 Facts Investigators Should Know[46]

The sociological perspective begins with one prominent demographic trend: family violence and violence against women is committed predominantly by men. While investigating a crime may not require one to be acquainted with the criminological theories, it is important to be familiar with trends. Trends and patterns can often lead an investigator in the right direction. Following are seventeen facts concerning violence against women and families that may be useful in the investigation of such crimes. Of course, as always, if an investigation turns up evidence of a crime, the local criminal justice authorities should be notified immediately.

1. In 1992, the American Medical Association reported that as many as one in three women will be assaulted by a domestic partner in her lifetime— 4 million in any given year. ("When Violence Hits Home," *Time*, June 4, 1994).
2. The average prison sentence of men who kill their women partners is two to six years. Women who kill their partners are, on average, sentenced to fifteen years. (National Coalition Against Domestic Violence, 1989).
3. Approximately one in ten high school students has experienced physical violence in dating relationships. Among college students, the figure rises to 22 percent (Gamache, 1991).
4. Police are more likely to respond within five minutes if an offender is a stranger than if an offender is known to a female victim. (Ronet Bachman, Ph.D., "Violence Against Women: A National Crime Victimization Survey Report." U.S. Department of Justice Bureau of Justice and Statistics, Jan. 1994, p. 9).
5. More than twice as many women are killed by their husbands or boyfriends as are murdered by strangers. (Arthur Kellerman, "Men, Women and Murder," *The Journal of Trauma*, July 17, 1992, pp. 1–5).
6. Among all female murder victims in 1992, 29 percent were slain by boyfriends or husbands; four percent of male victims were slain by their wives or girlfriends. (Federal Bureau of Investigations, 1993).
7. Women were attacked about six times more often by offenders with whom they had an intimate relationship than were male violence victims.
8. Nearly 30 percent of all female homicide victims were known to have been killed by their husbands, former husbands, or boyfriends. In contrast, just over three percent of male homicide victims were known to have been killed by their wives, former wives, or girlfriends. Husbands, former husbands, boyfriends and ex-boyfriends committed more than one million violent acts against women in 1995.
9. Family members or other people they knew committed more than 2.7 million violent crimes against women. Husbands, former husbands, boyfriends, and ex-boyfriends committed 26 percent of rapes and sexual assaults.
10. One third to one half of all children whose mothers are being abused are also being physically or sexually abused.
11. Forty-five percent of all violent attacks against female victims 12 years old and older by multiple offenders involve offenders they know.
12. The rate of intimate-offender attacks on women separated from their husbands was about three times higher than that of divorced women and about 25 times higher than that of married women.
13. Women of all races were equally vulnerable to attacks by intimates.

14. Female victims of violence were more likely to be injured when attacked by someone they knew than female victims of violence who were attacked by strangers.
15. Domestic violence costs United States businesses an estimated $3 to $5 billion annually due to interruptions of employee work.
16. More than 175,000 days were lost from paid work as a result of domestic assaults in 1980.
17. Some suggested readings:

> Daly, Martin, and Margo Wilson (1988). *Homicide*, Hawthorne, NY: Aldine de Gruyter.
>
> Gelles, Richard J., and Donileen Loeske (1993). *Controversies on Family Violence*, Newbury Park, CA: Sage Publications.
>
> Gelles, Richard J., and Murray A. Strauss (1988). *Intimate Violence*, New York: Simon & Schuster.
>
> Lystad, Mary (1986). *Violence in the Home: Interdisciplinary Perspectives*, New York: Brunner/Mazel.
>
> Strauss, Murray, Richard J. Gelles, and Suzanne K. Steinmetz (1980). *Behind Closed Doors: Violence in American Families*, New York: Doubleday.

55

File Maintenance[47]

In addition to regular investigative activities, most departments expend resources to develop leads or identify suspects by alternative means. For example, all departments maintain a variety of information files that serve as sources of investigative leads. These may include a file of crimes by type, location, or time period; a file of the addresses, descriptions, and modus operandi of known offenders; files of mug shots (usually organized by crime type and basic descriptors); files containing the fingerprints of all past arrestees; intelligence files with the names of individuals suspected of particular criminal activity; files of stolen or pawned property; and field interrogation files that indicate where and why certain individuals or vehicles were stopped, along with a description of the person and his or her vehicle. In addition, an increasing number of police agencies have highly developed crime analysis units that provide valuable information to investigators to help them narrow and focus their efforts.

In some departments, special details or strike forces are operated to provide investigative leads that never come through in normal incident reports. The most common example of such activity is a pawnshop detail that routinely inspects items taken in by pawnshops and compares them with lists of stolen property. Another type of strike force—typically called a "sting" operation—uses investigators to buy stolen property in an attempt to identify fences and burglars. In other cases, investigators are assigned temporarily as decoys in high-crime areas.

56

Follow Up (Latent) Investigation[48]

Steps taken after the preliminary investigation are part of the follow up (latent) investigation. New cases assigned to an investigator generally fall into one of three categories. Cases that receive first priority are those in which the investigative steps are obvious, based on the facts in the incident report. These are the cases in which the victim names a suspect, gives a license number, identifies where the suspect can be found, or indicates additional witnesses who were not interviewed by the responding patrol officer.

Second in priority are those cases that require attention not because of obvious leads, but because of the seriousness of the offense or its notoriety in the press or in the community. Investigators want to avoid charges by the community that they are not doing their job, or they may simply be outraged by an offense and want to help the victim. Cases of the lowest priority are routine cases that have no additional leads. In all departments, these cases are given only perfunctory treatment.

The first task of investigators when they come to work is to plan their activities for the day. Part of the morning is usually devoted to reviewing new cases, finishing paperwork, and making required court appearances. Late morning and afternoon are usually free for conducting interviews or other follow-up activities. The use of this "free" time is usually determined by a detective's own judgment; this judgment is based on a sense of priority about each case, the difficulty or attractiveness of conducting various interviews, and the activities of fellow investigators.

57

Force, The Use of[49]

The lawful and *safe* use of force by private personnel is a growing concern. Private security personnel are apt to encounter aggressive and potentially violent individuals in shopping centers, theaters, restaurants, amusement parks, "gated communities," and other places. In such environments, security personnel are largely taking the role of the old-time cop on the beat in a downtown urban environment. As there is more privitization of protective services in courthouses, municipal buildings, public parks, municipal garages, and housing projects, the potential for use of force encounters also rises.

USE OF FORCE CONTINUUM

Developed by Dr. Kevin Parsons, the Use of Force Continuum is a guide to using only that degree of force necessary to effect the immediate purpose for its employment. Other continuums have been developed by PPCT Management Systems, Larry Smith Enterprises, and others. All of them consist of a series of logical steps toward escalating the level of force used against an assailant. Officer presence would be followed by verbal controls which would be followed by soft empty hand control. After this would be striking with the hands, impact weapons, and finally, deadly force.

> Deadly Force: That force which is readily capable of causing death or *serious bodily injury*.
>
> Serious Bodily Injury: Bodily injury which creates a substantial risk of death or results in permanent disfigurement, or the protracted loss of use of any bodily member or organ.

EVALUATING THE USE OF FORCE

The following are some basic standards that courts use to evaluate the use of force by police and security personnel:

Ability: Does the person the officer is using force against have the ability to cause bodily harm to the officer or someone he/she has a duty to protect?

Opportunity: Does the assailant have the opportunity to assault at the instant of the use of force by the officer?

Jeopardy: Is the assailant placing the officer or others whom the officer has a duty to protect in imminent physical jeopardy?

Preclusion: Is the officer precluded from using force by taking some *alternative* action such as verbal persuasion, hard verbal commands, retreating, or the use of a lesser degree of force? As almost all encounters with persons do not call for the use of force, some attention to supportive communications is in order:

Honor subject's personal space

Introduce yourself

Employ *active listening* techniques

Use "we" rather than "you," which tends to be accusatory and inflammatory

Have subject sit down

Offer subject something to drink—other than hot coffee or alcoholic beverages!

Ask open-ended question which require some explanation by the subject

Use *paraphrasing* and *reflection* to clarify what the subject says

Beware of your fears and prejudices!

Some questions the officer can use to determine what, if any, force to employ in a given situation are:

- Am I in *imminent physical jeopardy*?
- Is someone whom I have a *duty* to protect in *imminent physical jeopardy?*
- Is my *mission* in jeopardy—preventing trespass, protecting assets from destruction, preventing theft, maintaining order, preventing escape?
- Do I have another *alternative*—persuasion, "hard" verbal techniques such as screaming, retreat, subsequent criminal or civil redress—to using force?
- How will my actions be viewed by others—supervisors, police, courts, the public/community—who may evaluate them?

SPECIFIC CIRCUMSTANCES

There are certain state statutes that enable private persons to use force in specific situations such as mental health commitments, in schools, where required by law to maintain order, and where persons are assembled. These statutes create both a legal justification for the use of force and a professional obligation. The obligation is not to be taken lightly! Officers should become familiar with local laws regarding this.

Juveniles

There are varied standards for using force when juveniles are involved. In many cases these statutes relate to the arrest of juveniles. State statutes on juveniles should be read and studied by those in the business of protection or teaching protection officers!

58

Force: The Use of by Private Citizens[50]

On occasion, private citizens, including security personnel, use either deadly or nondeadly physical force. This is done to protect themselves and others, to protect or recover their property, or to prevent crime. This should be of great concern to security managers, as they will hire others to protect corporate property. The user of force, and potentially the security manager and corporation, must justify not only the use of force but also the degree used in each particular instance. The key to using force lies in what is a reasonable response under the circumstances presented by the threat. One must take into consideration the seriousness, danger present, and kind and degree of the threatened misconduct. The more serious threat allows for the use of a higher degree of force than does a lesser threat and, of course, no security person should actually cause an escalation in the degree of force being used. Also, there is no need for any force to be used when the threat has subsided, except to make the apprehension.

One should consider that generally speaking life is worth more than property, that the law does not condone the use of unnecessary violence, and that one should use no more force than is necessary to accomplish one's purpose under the circumstances. Other considerations to think about before using force include determining: whether the threat is real, imminent, or pressing and accompanied by the ability to carry it out; whether there are alternatives to using force; how much time has elapsed since the incident occurred; whether force to be used is for retaliatory purposes only; and who actually is the provocateur or aggressor. Remember that the amount of force used by an employee may be measured at a much later date by others—namely by a jury. Also note that many states have statutes covering the permissible limits on the use of force.

59

Freedom of Information Act

The Federal Freedom of Information Act (FOIA) applies to documents held by agencies in the executive branch of the federal government. The executive branch includes cabinet departments, military departments, government corporations and/or those controlled by the government, independent regulatory agencies, and any others within the executive branch.

The FOIA does not apply to elected officials of the federal government, the vice president, senators, congressmen, or members of the federal judiciary. The FOIA does not apply to private companies, persons who receive federal contracts or grants, tax exempt organizations, or state and local governments.

All states and some local governments have passed laws like the FOIA that allow people to request access to records. There are additional state and federal laws that allow or permit access to documents in the possession of organizations not covered by the federal FOIA.

Personal notes of agency employees may not be considered agency records. Any records that are not agency records are not available under the FOIA. The FOIA does not define agency records, but any records or material that is in the possession or care/custody/control of the agency is considered to be an agency record.

A requester may ask for records as opposed to asking for information. Simply put, you may not ask to see "all your twos." You must ask to see "the inventory of the twos of hearts." This means that an agency is required to look for an existing record or document in response to a request. They are not required to do research, create a new record, or collect information they do not already have.

All requests must be specific and carefully composed in order to obtain the information you seek. The law demands that the requestor reasonably describe the records or information being sought. It must be understood that different agencies have different methods of maintaining records or retrieving material.

When making a request under the FOIA you must be specific as to the agency that has the records you want. The request must be in writing and addressed to the attention of the FOIA officer of that particular agency. You start by stating that your request is based upon the FOIA. You would then state the specific records or information you want, and you must identify yourself fully and with complete detail. It is strongly suggested that you keep a copy of your request for follow-up purposes. FOIA requestors may have to pay a fee for all or some of the costs of assembling the data. In the case of a small or noncommercial request the fee may be waived.

The Office of Information and Privacy (OIP) is the official point of contact in the executive branch for advice and policy determinations pertaining to the FOIA. You may contact the OIP-FOIA Counselor Service for help. There is a complete listing for the numerous agencies and departments.

There are Federal Information Centers located in over forty metropolitan areas all across our country. They can assist you and smooth the way to minimize frustration and disappointment when trying to obtain information.

60

The Grand Jury: What Is It?

The successful efforts of an investigator when supported by decision makers can frequently culminate in a grand jury proceeding. We have experienced numerous misconceptions and often unsuccessful presentations as a result of not fully understanding the process. Just what is a grand jury anyway?

The early American colonists brought the concept with them from England and it was incorporated into the United States Constitution by our forefathers. Simply put, the grand jury is meant to provide a fair and impartial determination concerning criminal acts known or suspected to have been committed by a person or persons as in conspiracies involving white collar crime. While a grand jury is supposed to be impartial and independent, it is controlled by the court and under the direction of the prosecutor.

There are basically two specific functions of the grand jury process. These are:

1. To ascertain if there is probable cause that a crime exists or has been committed.
2. To protect citizens from false prosecutions. This is hard for many to comprehend as the general conception is that the grand jury is a tool of the prosecutor. Many feel it is part of the court system since it depends on the subpoena process of the courts to get witnesses to testify. The Fifth Amendment of the United States Constitution states that "no person shall be held to answer for a capital, or otherwise infamous crime unless upon presentment or indictment of a grand jury."

The Federal Rules of Criminal Procedure, Rule 6(a) authorizes the courts to impanel as many grand juries as necessary to serve the public interest. There are two types of grand juries. These are:

- A regular grand jury is usually impaneled for a month but can serve up to eighteen months. There are allowances for up to a six month extension if necessary as in some complicated conspiracy cases.
- A special grand jury serves on selected irregular days for up to eighteen months, but may also be extended for three additional periods of up to six months each.

It should be noted that there is no difference between the regular and special grand juries other than the allowable time served including possible extensions.

The grand jury on the basis of their deliberations and review of the evidence and facts presented by the prosecutor, votes to promote a formal written accusation of having committed a crime. This is called an *indictment* and is prepared and written by the prosecutor.

In view of the special prosecutor's actions with the federal grand jury concerned with hearing evidence in the investigation of President William Jefferson Clinton during 1997–2000, it is with some confusion that we address the topic of grand jury secrecy. The practice of grand jury secrecy is covered and firmly established in the Federal Rules of Criminal Procedure, Rule 6(e), where it states that all involved with grand jury proceedings, including typists and stenographers, "shall not disclose matters occurring before the grand jury." To violate secrecy is to be considered in contempt of court. There are allowances for disclosing grand jury material without court permission, depending upon the context and to whom it is disclosed. An example of this is for a specific judicial proceeding with evidence of a specific need.

This discussion only begins to cover all of the information concerning grand jury concerns. Complete data is available in the Federal Rules of Criminal Procedure.

61

Gunshot Cases: 9 Common Errors of Observation and Interpretation

1. Failure to perform a complete autopsy
2. Nonrecognition of gunshot wounds in obscure or unexpected locations (mouth, eye, vagina, axilla) and in burned or decomposed bodies
3. Failure to utilize x-ray or fluoroscopy for location of bone injuries or missiles
4. Misinterpretation of lacerated (explosive) contact wounds as exit wounds (or blunt force injuries)
5. Failure to examine bullets for evidence of ricochet
6. Misinterpretation of grease and other bullet fouling as powder residue
7. Incorrect identification of the larger of paired wounds as the exit wound merely because of its size
8. Incorrect identification of the exit wound having marginal abrasion, caused by pressure on skin upon exit of missile, as a wound of entrance
9. Premature release of information before correlating all investigative, autopsy, and laboratory findings

62

Hate Crimes: A Policymaker's Guide[51]

WHAT IS A HATE CRIME?

For the purposes of this monograph, hate crimes, or bias-motivated crimes, are defined as offenses motivated by hatred against a victim based on his or her race, religion, sexual orientation, handicap, ethnicity, or national origin. While such a definition may make identifying a hate crime seem like a simple task, criminal acts motivated by bias can easily be confused with forms of expression protected by the U.S. Constitution.

WHAT MAKES HATE CRIMES DIFFERENT FROM OTHER CRIMES?

The number of hate crimes may seem small when compared with the incidents of other types of crimes in the United States. In 1993, for example, 11 of the 24,536 murders reported in the United States were classified as hate crimes, as were 13 of the 104,806 reported rapes. But the simple truth about hate crimes is that each offense victimizes not one victim but many. A hate crime victimizes not only the immediate target but every member of the group that the immediate target represents. A bias-motivated offense can cause a broad ripple of discomfiture among members of a targeted group, and a violent hate crime can act like a virus, quickly spreading feelings of terror and loathing across an entire community. Apart from their psychological impacts, violent hate crimes can create tides of retaliation and counter-retaliation. Therefore, criminal acts motivated by bias may carry far more weight than other types of criminal acts.

CAUSES AND CHARACTERISTICS OF HATE CRIMES

A host of factors may create a climate in which people, motivated by their biases, take criminal action. Such factors include poor or uncertain economic conditions, racial stereotypes in films and on television, hate filled discourse on talk shows or in political advertisements, the use of racial code language such as "welfare mothers" and "inner city thugs," and an individual's personal experiences with members of particular minority groups. Once a climate of hate is created, a single incident—such as the videotaped beating of Los Angeles, California, motorist Rodney King—can trigger a wave of hate crimes.

HATE CRIME VICTIMS

African Americans, who constitute the single largest minority group in the nation, are more likely to be targets of hate crimes than members of any other group. Of the nearly 8,000 hate crimes reported in 1995, almost 3,000 of them were motivated by bias against African Americans. Other typical victims were Jews, homosexuals, Muslims, and increasingly, Asian Americans.

HATE CRIME PERPETRATORS

Most hate crimes are committed not by members of an organized hate group but by individual citizens. Some perpetrators resent the growing economic power of a particular racial or ethnic group and engage in "scapegoating"; others react to a perceived threat to the safety and property value of their neighborhood. Still other offenders include "thrill seekers"—those who randomly target interchangeable representatives of minority groups for harassment and violence, and "mission offenders"—those who believe they are on a mission to rid the world of some perceived evil. This last group accounts for a tiny percentage of bias-motivated offenders. The majority of offenders—and passive observers—are merely individuals who believe racial and ethnic stereotypes and act on spur-of-the-moment impulses. Frequently, alcohol or drug use is a factor in the commission of hate crimes.

63

The Homicide Investigator

"No greater honor will ever be bestowed on an Officer or a more profound duty imposed on him than when he is entrusted with the investigation of the death of a human being. It is his duty to find the facts regardless of color or creed without prejudice, and to let no power on earth deter him from presenting these facts to the court without regard to personality" (FBI Academy, Quantico, VA).

64

The Homicide Victim: 70 Things You Should Know

This is a checklist of questions concerning the details of a victim's background and activities—any of which may prove useful in establishing a link with the perpetrator. This list may also be useful in establishing a *common denominator* where there has been more than one homicide and the cases may be connected.

1. Victim's full name
2. Sex
3. Race
4. Date of birth
5. Place of birth
6. Nickname
7. Maiden or previous name used
8. Height
9. Weight
10. Hair—length, color, style
11. Physical defects
12. Wear glasses? Doctor, optometrist
13. Wear dentures? Dentist?
14. Marital status; if divorced, former spouse's name
15. Children's names, ages, locations
16. Present employment, reason for change
17. Former employment, reason for change
18. Employment bureaus or services used
19. Union or trade organizations
20. Military history. If rejected, why?
21. Doctors—names, addresses, specialties, case histories

22. Hospital records
23. Druggist frequented
24. Insurance—companies, types of coverage, beneficiary, burial plans
25. Financial status—banks, safe deposits, loans, stocks, bonds
26. Accountant
27. Present address
28. Former addresses—dates there
29. Criminal record—traffic record (accidents, etc.)
30. Check newspaper morgues for any stories on victim
31. Did victim call for any police services?
32. Did victim call for any fire services?
33. Did victim mention any strange mail or phone calls?
34. Complete history of education—dates, locations
35. Churches, religion, past and present
36. Clubs, organizations—meeting dates, locations
37. Habits—drinking, gambling, movies, restaurants, around home
38. Hobbies, sports
39. Automobile—description, where and when bought, salesman
40. Automobile repairs, servicing, gas
41. Usual mode of travel
42. Any key service—car, home, details
43. Home services—telephone, electric, gas, water
44. Home repairs—additions, remodeling
45. Yard work
46. Recent purchases of appliances, furniture, and so on. When, where, and how delivered
47. Magazine salesmen
48. Postmen
49. Trashmen
50. Any solicitors in area recently?
51. Any photographs taken recently? Where, by whom?
52. Any deaths in family recently? Where, how, what funeral home?
53. List all friends, acquaintances, old and new
54. Pets—vets, pet stores
55. Jury duty in past?
56. Trips, business or pleasure—where, why, with who?
57. Usual type of outer clothing worn
58. Usual type of inner clothing worn
59. Clothing store frequented
60. Department store frequented
61. Telephone, beeper, fax line, cell phone
62. Shoe repair shop, shoe stores
63. Jewelry store or repair shop
64. Library frequented
65. Barber or beauty shop used
66. Grocery store frequented

67. Any other type store frequented
68. Internet activity
69. Computer's hard drive
70. Enemies

65

Implications for Public Action[52]

First, it is clear that programs must be founded in fact. Information must be used to enhance cooperative efforts. Facts must replace unsubstantiated beliefs in determining program approaches. Second, popular theories of criminal behavior have to be viewed in terms of the failure of social, psychological, and biological theories to explain the broad range of criminal activity throughout all levels of our society. This means that what we do know has to be used, while we await further information from science. Supervision, control, interagency cooperation, and environmental management are known capabilities. Finally, the statistics about crime and victimization in public housing must be considered to be the tip of the iceberg in terms of a real understanding of the problem. This also means that the relationship between the developmental activities and the contiguous neighborhood has to be defined and taken into account in planning.

Uncontrolled criminal activity in public areas, especially housing, affects the quality of life in the project. It affects the perceptions and the subsequent development of attitudes and behavior of the children who grow up in these places. It affects the neighborhood. Can a healthy neighborhood absorb a public housing project and make it part of its social fabric? Can a project reach out to a troubled neighborhood and become the focal point for neighborhood development? These questions must and can be answered in a well-controlled and fundamentally CPTED (Crime Prevention Through Environmental Design) neighborhood project.

Young people experience problems that go beyond traditional concepts of crime and victimization. Young people under 24 years account for about 51 percent of all arrests. Young people under the age of 18 account for 17 percent of all arrests and about 40 percent of all arrests for serious property crimes. Some more startling facts include:

- Persons under age 18 are the most highly victimized segment of our population.
- Persons under age 18 are the least likely segment of our population to report a criminal victimization.
- Persons under age 18 are seven times more likely to be victimized by another young person than by an adult.
- Suburban youth experience a school dropout rate of 25 percent and urban youth a dropout rate of 35 percent.
- Child molestation and abuse is immeasurable, but it is estimated that 1,100 children died as a result of neglect in 1986.
- Drug and alcohol use are common for elementary, middle and high school students—7 percent of eighth-grade students used marijuana by grade six; 62 percent of eighth-grade students who reported having tried cocaine said that they tried it first in grade seven.
- High school seniors reported (1986) having used drugs in 57 percent of all interview responses.
- Thirty-five percent of all boys age 0–18 will be arrested at least once; 18–21 of these young men will become career offenders.

Young people under age 18 represent only 27 percent of the American population. Yet, this same age group is commonly more than 50 percent of the population of public housing projects. Habitual offender programs have estimated that a disproportionate number (per capita) of officially identified habitual juvenile offenders reside in public housing, in contrast to other housing forms.

66

Incident Reports and Preliminary Investigations[53]

Most cases involving the discovery of major felonies are initiated by citizens who call the police to report the crime or by a police patrol unit that responds to evidence that a crime is in progress. In either case, the first police representative on the scene is usually a uniformed patrol officer. The patrol officer's duties are to provide aid to the victim, to secure the crime scene for later investigation, and to document the facts of the crime. In a few departments, investigators may be dispatched simultaneously with the patrol unit to begin an investigation of the crime, but in most departments, investigation by detectives does not take place until after a patrol officer files a report. The patrol officer's initial report usually contains the basic facts of the crime—the identity of the victim, a description of the suspect, the identity and location of any potential witnesses, a description of the crime scene, and any pertinent statements by witnesses or the victim. This report is passed on to the detective unit, which then continues the investigation.

Patrol units are generally under considerable pressure to cut short their investigations and get back on patrol. Thus detectives, rather than patrol officers, are usually responsible for developing potential leads and continuing the investigation. In some departments, however, patrol officers are encouraged to use their own initiative to continue an investigation, perhaps by conducting house-to-house checks or using other means to track down suspects.

67

Informants

Investigative information may be learned or obtained from three types of people.

1. Honest and caring employees and/or law abiding citizens. These can be anyone in your employ or with whom you associate or trade either in business or private life.
2. The true informers, who are motivated by fear of the law or because they are in trouble with the authorities. A short definition of *informer* is someone who gains information because of a definite personal gain or motive. The motivations to offer information or inform on someone or something are varied. Generally, they fall into these categories: revenge, reward, repentance and, at times, ego.
3. The types of individuals who are considered eccentric or nuisances. This category is frequently known as a busybody or gossip. Included in this area are also those persons who may be able to function in normal life situations but are inhibited in some capacity.

Using an informant is generally recommended when it is difficult or impossible to make observations or obtain information yourself. They are the conduit for data that is simply not available through any other legitimate means. It must be stressed that informants can very often be difficult to control and can become a source of embarrassment. It must be understood that great care must be taken to protect and safeguard the identity of your informant or source of information. Never compromise or disclose your source. Information obtained from an informer must be tested and reproven by other means in order to test, protect, and use the data. Verify everything that is possible to use.

Be truthful with your sources and make no promises you do not or cannot keep. There can be no tolerance of criminal involvement or even the appearance of criminal involvement on the part of yourself or your source. You must constantly evaluate the motives and/or hidden agendas of your informants when estimating their reliability.

There are two constants when dealing with specific sources of information:

1. Anonymous telephone informants very rarely call back. Get all the data you can at the time of the call.
2. Anonymous correspondence is generally written by cranks and rarely leads to any substantial investigation. However, each letter must be considered and evaluated.

68

Intent[54]

In cases in which undercover agents are trying to lay the basis for a criminal prosecution, they must avoid originating the crime or the criminal intent. For example, if an undercover agent asks another employee to steal an article, entrapment would probably be a successful defense against criminal charges.

How far can a private undercover agent go in roping a suspect? Although the final test of an agent's activities must be met in court, many lawyers feel that the general rule of entrapment permits the following conservative acts:

1. Assisting the suspect in the theft of goods if the theft is first suggested by the suspect, who requests the agent's assistance

2. Giving the suspect opportunities to steal goods
3. Subtly suggesting knowledge of theft activities to induce the suspect to confide in the agent
4. Inquiring about methods of stealing goods in order to discover the suspect's modus operandi and to ascertain facts that will enable the agent to catch the suspect in the act of stealing

In addition to these four examples, there are probably a number of other cooperative activities that an undercover agent may perform to build a theft case, as long as the theft itself does not originate with the agent.

One factor to keep in mind when reviewing these guidelines is that they are all directed toward criminal prosecutions. Private companies should never dissuade undercover agents from breaking theft rings and uncovering dishonest employees, even when the agent's activities might subsequently rule out a successful criminal prosecution. Even when the rules of criminal evidence cannot be satisfied, an operative might be able to break a case, obtaining confessions and other facts that support the discharge of dishonest employees.

Company security efforts should not be confined primarily to conformance to criminal rules of evidence. If this were the case, companies would not realize the full value of a security force, particularly in the prevention of losses through the early discovery of the activities of dishonest employees. A company's primary objective in any theft case should be the separation of the offender from the payroll. Successful prosecution should be only a secondary objective.

In addition, many aggressive law enforcement agencies do not seem to be too concerned with the rule of entrapment. Many successful undercover investigations probably skirt very close to a technical violation of the general rule.

69

Internal Theft[55]

Internal theft is one of the more difficult types of crimes to solve. For example, you return to your complex January 2nd. The department has been closed down for nine days. Four computers and programs are missing as well as the petty cash. There are no fingerprints, no breaking of doors or windows, and the alarm was turned on December 23rd. Four thousand dollars was stolen from the office safe.

Two people have combinations. One of the two was away for the weekend. Investigations showed the combination number was kept in a Rolodex under "S".

The following is a checklist to assist you in reviewing the "Internal Theft Controls."

- Is a cashier's fund also counted and verified by management?
- Are proper security measures taken when a cashier has to turn in or pick up money from management?
- Do the cashiers have a register cash count form that has been completed?
- Are all cashiers assigned to use only one register exclusively?
- Is each cashier issued a unique pass code or ID number to activate the register and prevent anyone else from using it?
- Are control keys for cash register functions only given to management?
- Do all voids, post-voids and refunds over $20 require management approval before these transactions are processed?
- Are overages and shortages constantly monitored and investigated?
- Are excessive amounts of "No Sale" transactions investigated?
- Are all "No Sale" and void receipts turned in with the rest of a cashier's daily paperwork?
- Are all cashiers and salespeople periodically integrity (honesty) shopped with a unique product purchased with the exact amount to verify that the transaction was rung up correctly?
- During the integrity shop, are receipts intentionally left behind to see if they show up as voids or refunds later on?
- Are all integrity shops thoroughly and completely documented with specific items, amounts, registers, times, conversations, and cashiers/salespeople in case of their use in a theft prosecution?
- Has management noticed any unusual interaction between employees working at registers and customers?
- Is there a reason written on the back of "No Sale" and voids receipts?
- Are all voided transactions followed by a "No Sale" thoroughly investigated?
- Do all refunds require the original merchandise and receipt before being processed?
- Does the refund voucher contain the following elements:
    Customer's address, home and work phone
    Date of return
    Store/business location
    The employee who prepared the refund voucher
    Type of refund—cash, store check, bank card, store credit
    Transaction/invoice number of original sale
    Date and location of original sale
    Management signature approval
    Amount approved by management for the total refund
    Stock number (SKU) and quantity of merchandise
    Description of the merchandise returned
    A list price of each item returned

Sequentially numbered refund forms
Customer's signature
Customer's driver's license number
Three part carbon refund form

- If an individual doesn't have the original sales receipt is the refund claim forwarded to the company's loss prevention department for investigation of its validity?
- Does loss prevention issue a check to the customer only after the claim has been determined to be legitimate?
- Is there a list or database of known fraudulent refund artists directly available to all personnel who handle refund claims?
- When employees are processing a refund claim, do they first place the merchandise out of the customer's reach in case of an attempted fraudulent return?
- Do employees fill out an incident report form for all suspected fraudulent returns?
- Do employees inform individuals with suspected fraudulent return claims and no receipts that the sale must be researched at the corporate office and then a check will be issued for the refund?
- Are employees alerted to suspected fraudulent returns by incomplete information such as addresses, phone numbers, no ID, original sale information, or vague reason for return?
- Are employees alerted to possibly fraudulent claims by customers who exhibit nervous behavior, create a "scene," are in a hurry, are overly nice or attempt to distract the employee, or who have someone waiting for them in a car running out in the parking lot?
- Are employees alerted to attempted fraudulent returns using another store's receipt (within the same chain)?
- Are employees alerted to attempted fraudulent returns using altered or color photocopied receipts with shoplifted merchandise?
- Is all daily paperwork (such as cash counts, transaction totals, bank card vouchers, correction/adjustment sheets, copies of refund forms, sales invoices, etc.) forwarded daily to a sales audit department or individual?
- Are bank deposits made daily?
- Are all employees bonded?
- Are employees' time cards randomly audited to verify their accuracy?
- Are random register audits performed on all employees on a regular, yet unpredictable, basis?
- Is covert surveillance used to detect under-ringing and failures to charge for items?
- Is a cashier register interface with CCTV incorporated to directly observe and videotape a cashier's performance to possibly be used as evidence if theft is detected?
- Are marking guns kept in a secure location?
- Is there a periodic physical inventory and audit for all merchandise, supplies, and equipment?

- Are these inventories conducted by an outside, independent firm?
- If inventories are done internally, are individuals who do not work directly with these areas used?
- Is double-counting done by two separate persons during the inventory to ensure accuracy?
- Are all variances and discrepancies in inventories immediately investigated?

70

International Intelligence Network: Investigations and Security

INTELNET is a unique multinational network of licensed private investigators and expert consulting personnel with superior expertise in security and loss prevention. These professional specialists provide investigative and consultative services to a broad spectrum of attorneys, business, industry, government agencies, and institutions. These experts, most with investigative and security related backgrounds from previous service in military, federal, state, and local law enforcement agencies, are identified as to specialty and location through their membership in INTELNET, which is the focal point for the organization.

Each INTELNET member is an independent businessperson, operating his or her enterprise. INTELNET members adhere to the INTELNET Code of Conduct, which stresses ethical, professional, and expert conduct. Their capabilities, reputation, and performance are sustained through their membership in INTELNET, and enhanced by their participation in the seminars, training, and experiences available from the INTELNET organization and other related associations.

INTELNET members number over 350, with at least one in every state. In addition, there are now members in over 30 foreign countries, including Eastern European nations, the Pacific rim, Central and South America, Africa, and the Middle East.

If you have any questions for Jim Carino, Executive Director of INTELNET, you can contact him at:

INTELNET
P.O. Box 350
Gladwyne, PA 19035
Phone: (610) 525-1097 or (800) 784-2020
Fax: (215) 781-3575

71

The Internet[56]

The Internet has become an important topic in recent years, and its importance to society, business, and government agencies is expected to increase. Therefore, it will also increase in importance to the twenty-first-century ISSO.

The major technological change making the Internet possible has been the expansion of networks nationally and internationally. These networks increasingly have gained in importance due to their use and major communication links and international business links. The backbone of the international network structure has been increasing the access to and use of Internet, which is the major communication and business tool of global commerce. It will continue to expand, as will the world's use of it.

72

The Internet's Impact on Crime[57]

Crime on the Internet will continue to increase in amount and sophistication as more people around the world gain access to it. It is fast becoming an international technocrime tool. Each system connected to the Internet is subject to attack, and many have been attacked. These attacks are growing in both their sophistication and number.

Law enforcement officers are hampered in investigating such attacks by nonexistent laws, lack of jurisdiction, and difficulty in getting cooperation from law enforcement officers of other countries because of politics, different laws, and so forth. For example, what may be illegal in Indonesia may not be illegal in the Netherlands. Therefore, extradition would be impossible, since the citizen of the Netherlands violated no law of his or her country. The investigation of technocrimes is complicated enough; when these crimes are accomplished internationally, it is almost impossible to bring the criminals to justice.

WHO ARE THE CULPRITS?

The history of technocrime cases has shown that these criminals include, but are not limited to:

1. Internal employees
2. Consultants and temporary employees
3. Hackers, phreakers, and crackers
4. Radicals and terrorists
5. Professional technocriminals for hire

RISKS DUE TO THE INTERNET

There are many reasons for these risks, such as:

1. Global economic competition, where industrial and economic espionage can be conducted with little risk of being caught
2. The decline of the mainframe system, the increase in LANs and WANs, and the creation of client-server systems—all of which rely more on the users to

protect the systems and information than on a professional staff of systems personnel

3. The "Maginot line" mentality of managers and some InfoSec staff members, who look at access control software, firewalls, and passwords as the only security needed

4. The focus on customer service by network staffs as the highest priority, as well as technical staffs' lack of familiarity with their security role

5. Limited security technology

The Internet security answer for transmission of information appears to be encryption. Encryption today seems to be in a position similar to the locks of the 1800s. Then, knowledge of locks was available only to experts. Criminals needed keys to break in and concentrated on obtaining keys. With the invention of powerful explosives, keys were no longer needed—the criminals just blew off the locks.

The same may be true in the future with encryption, but as we have begun to see, encryption works because guessing the right key, statistically at least, is almost impossible. But what if a person did guess it—even guessed it the first time? Also, the more tries at guessing the encryption key, the better are your statistical chances of getting it right. The real problem with encryption is key management, just as we have password management today. Also, with more powerful and cheaper computers, criminals are finding that they can identify encryption keys.

Encryption can protect, with some degree of success, our ability to secure our mail. However, it cannot prevent denial of service, a growing threat.

HOW TO PROTECT THE ORGANIZATION

To protect the corporation or government agency from the Internet problems, the ISSO must have close surveillance of their connections to the Internet itself. Firewall systems must be used to help protect internal networks, routers, and internal firewalls to compartmentalize nodes and security systems for all servers. One-time passwords still may be used but will eventually give way to more bio-medical forms of identification such as retina scans or voice prints. As InfoSec technology becomes more sophisticated, firewalls probably will be integrated with other pieces of hardware and software, thus providing not only InfoSec but also information throughput and processing. The InfoSec approach is a layered approach, so do not think firewalls are the total answer. Remember IP spoofing and sendmail vulnerabilities?

The Internet will continue expansion to individuals, businesses, and government agencies throughout the world and will do so exponentially. There will be more reliance for contract negotiations and formal contract agreements through the Internet, paving the way for some serious legal issues and contract frauds. To meet the challenge, the ISSO must understand the Internet and its potential use as a tool as well as the harm it could cause.

73

The Internet and the World Wide Web

There are numerous research and investigative aids accessible to investigations on the Internet and the World Wide Web (WWW). The Internet is a collection of computer networks. Examples of these are CompuServe and America On-Line. There is information available on bulletin board systems (BBS), that is stored electronically and accessible by individual contact. This later is a cumbersome method as the BBSs are not joined together but each has to be accessed independently. The Internet is all interconnected and once you access the World Wide Web you can transfer/connect to all other World Wide Web sites. All of this starts with a local phone call.

Each site on the net has a Uniform Resource Locator (URL). The specific means by which you travel to the URLs are called *protocols*. Investigative research URLs include the following:

- FTP:ftp://.whitehouse.gov/pub
- www.news.com

  News groups:

- www.msnbc.com
- www.cnbc.com
- www.cnn.com
- www.usatoday.com

  Sites for research and data helpful to investigators include:

- www.background.com (association)
- www.bh.com (publisher)
- www.yahoo.com (resource)
- www.excite.com (resource)
- www.infoseek.com (search)
- www.info.gov/ (government information exchange)
- www.census.gov/ (U.S. Census Bureau)
- www.counterpoint.com (federal regulations)
- www.fedworld.gov/supcourt (Supreme Court)
- http://fairuse.stanford.edu/ (copyright information)

- http://www.law.com (Institute of Criminology)
- www.inta.org/ (trademark association)

    Some additional useful sites are:

- www.litigationconsultants.com (expert witnesses)
- www.ifpo.com (multi site)
- www.securitymanagement.com (magazine)
- www.ncsa.com (association)
- www.calibrepress.com (multi site)

74

Interviewing and Interrogating

The greatest source of investigative information is the spoken word. Until every witness, victim, or suspect associated with an investigation has been interviewed, no investigation should be considered complete. Efficient interviewing or questioning techniques are not learned from polite society, ordinary schools, or experience. It is a learned skill that must be acquired by specialized training and further developed through experience.

A good investigator should develop his or her intuition of when and how to proceed when conducting an interview or interrogation. This is the case regai 1-less of the extent of the investigator's formalized training and skills developmen . Such a spontaneous judgment does have the possible shortcoming of coming to a conclusion without necessarily evaluating all the variables. This risk does not preclude highly successful interviewing skills when the innate skills and experience are obtained. However, anything that can be learned through trial and error methods can be learned through skills, training, and development more quickly.

Remember, under no circumstances or conditions can abuse, threats, harassment, coercion, and intimidation be used or suggested when conducting an interview or interrogation. It is permissible, however, to use systematic persuasion in a humane and friendly atmosphere. You are trying to wear down the inhibitions of the individual by logic and the natural incentives to cooperative. You are making the subject feel that cooperating and telling the truth will benefit him or her.

It is important to accept that people are generally the best source of information. Somebody usually knows all of the important details of the object or cause of an investigation. It is also usual that a good many others will have enough knowledge to enable you to piece the facts together. When you effectively get the information from all involved, you generally can successfully conclude an investigation.

75

Interviewing: Code of Ethic[58]

- To verify the truth fairly, impartially, and objectively
- To make no false statements and claims regarding personal qualifications
- To maintain the highest standards of moral, ethical, and professional conduct
- To be governed by laws of equity and justice in the performance of all duties
- To respect the inherent dignity of all people
- To be just, fair, and impartial with each individual, irrespective of social, political, racial, ethnic, or religious group, economic status, or physical characteristics
- To discharge professional duties and obligations with independence, dignity, and self-respect
- To keep all decisions and reports scrupulously free of any personal, financial, political, fraternal, social, or improper influence
- To refrain from false or misleading reporting
- To accept no illegal or improper remuneration for services rendered
- To refrain from representing competing or conflicting interests when such representation is, or gives the appearance of being, unethical
- To refrain from slanderous or libelous public criticism of the law enforcement profession or its membership, by recognizing that the welfare and advancement of the profession and society supersede personal desires and ambitions
- To recommend and accept for membership in the profession those who strive in every way to be a credit to the profession
- To support the purposes and objectives of the law enforcement profession

76

Interviewing in White Collar Crime

Frequently, when developing an investigation with a specific suspect in mind it is necessary to develop a financial profile. It is important then to establish if the value of his or her assets far exceed the obvious sources of legitimate income or compensation. Your goal is to establish a motive for the crime and to show that illegal payments or funds were obtained.

Your suspect must be interviewed first about the source of money and other assets. Where are their savings and bank accounts, property(s), vehicles and recreational equipment, investments, and does their style and manner of living match their legitimate income? During the interview, your goal is to establish that he or she has resources and assets far in excess of reasonable or legitimate sources. Allowing the suspect to explain their sources of cash on hand or assets may develop leads that can be disproved as legitimate sources for the funds or assets. The more information you obtain during the interview the easier it may be to establish that the suspect lied or was concealing information. The likelihood that the suspect may give partial admissions is enhanced if during the interview you ask questions that have no application to the specific crime. Questions that are nonthreatening to the suspect may be asked before slipping in a very direct and important one. You are trying to establish that the suspect has lied or concealed income and cannot explain income or assets.

77

Invasion of Privacy[59]

Invasion of privacy deals with the right of individuals to withhold themselves or their property from public scrutiny, if they so choose. It is the right to be left alone. There are four general classes of tort actions for invasion of privacy:

1. Appropriation of the plaintiff's name or likeness to the benefit or advantage of the defendant
2. Intrusion upon the seclusion or solitude of the plaintiff by invading his home or eavesdropping
3. The public disclosure of private facts
4. Publicity that places the plaintiff in a false light in the public eye

A security manager should be most concerned with number 2, intrusion upon seclusion or solitude. The concern comes about because of the great amount of investigative activity conducted by the private security industry. The right to privacy is a personal right, and the invasion of that right is a willful tort that constitutes a legal injury. Physical intrusion, analogous to trespass, is the unwarranted invasion to the right of privacy when highly offensive and objectionable to the reasonable person. Surveillance may be so overzealous as to render it actionable in a court of law. It is the right of every citizen to be left alone. Intrusion is wrongful when it is outrageous and causes mental suffering, shame, and humiliation to a person of ordinary sensibilities.

While the right of privacy may be waived by one who files an action for damages resulting from a tort, it is only waived to the extent of the defendant's intervening right to investigate and ascertain for himself the true state of the injury. The waiver is only for a reasonably unobtrusive type of investigation that would be in the defendant's interest in preparing its case. Overt, extended and prolonged activities, such as trailing in a conspicuous manner sufficient to excite speculation in the neighbors, constant following in public places, pursuit tactics openly conducted late at night so as to alarm the average person, coupled with other acts amounting to trespass and eavesdropping, which resulted in fright, shock, and physical and mental impairment, are not reasonable conduct within the bounds of the implied waiver.

78

Investigative Chemicals

Investigative or de facto chemicals are substances that are inconspicuous but have chemical and physical properties that can be easily identified. Generally, these are in one of three forms: powder, liquid, or pencil. When placed on objects or materials and even humans, they can serve as either a visible or invisible identification method.

The applications for the use of chemicals include the following:

- To identify people who enter prohibited/restricted areas
- To identify those persons handling unauthorized objects
- To identify money or negotiables used in criminal transactions
- To be able to identify writing and/or publishing inks, gasoline, or other liquids and documents

The various types of chemicals include the following:

- *Fluorescein*: Forms a maroon powder which produces a yellow stain when it comes in contact with water. When exposed to ultraviolet light it gives a bright yellow glow. It is easy to wash off.
- *Eosine*: As above, but produces a red powder and leaves a red stain. It adheres to objects very well and is difficult to wash off.
- *Rhodamine B*: This brown powder, when contacted by water, will leave a cherry colored stain and when subjected to ultraviolet light will give an orange color. It is difficult to wash off.
- *Magenta Fuchsin*: This is a fine, dark green powder that will produce a very vivid red stain when contacted by water that is very difficult to wash off.
- *Malachite Green*: Used in a fine, green powder form, it produces a blue-green stain when touched by water. It adheres moderately well and it is extremely difficult to wash off.
- *Crystal Violet*: When used in green powder form, it will produce a violet stain when touched by water. It adheres to objects very well and is very difficult to remove.
- *Anthracene*: Coal tar hydrocarbon in pencil or powder form that is difficult to wash off and gives off a brilliant fluorescence under ultraviolet light.
- *Fluorene*: This also is a coal tar hydrocarbon with strong fluorescent abilities. It may be used to identify gasoline and other solutions.

79

The "Sloppy" Investigation

Simply put, this is the complete opposite of an acceptable professional investigation: one in which leads are not thoroughly documented and/or checked; personal bias and prejudice of the investigator slips into the process of data collection; no successful completion whereby a discharge, arrest, or complaint is made; evidence is overlooked and poorly or improperly handled; and finally, there is inept selection of the resources to investigate the particular investigation.

In view of our mutual experiences and past involvement with the process of investigations, we have never observed anything written on the subject but have acknowledged that many investigations were "sloppy" and poorly managed. Principal responsibility for a professional or "good" investigation rests with the investigator or case manager. Frequently, the case manager may be the only resource assigned to the investigation. The manager is accountable for the quality of his or her efforts or the efforts by all involved. The manager or supervisor must read and review every report, every piece of evidence and documentation, interview the people, and evaluate the resources assigned or involved with the investigative effort.

Example: A supervisor reviewing a well written and apparently complete investigation of a safe that had been locked on a Friday evening with $400.00 inside. On Monday morning the money was missing. The assigned investigator had identified two suspects. The case reviewer inquired about the safe manufacturer and reputation. It was determined that the safe in question could be "cracked" by even the most inexperienced thief.

Example: A clerk responsible for petty cash disbursement goes off on vacation. Upon returning, she determines that the cash is missing. The investigator found no suspects and no forced entry. It was later determined that the secretary next to the clerk never locked her desk and a duplicate key was kept in the desk tray.

Example: Wrong numbers were assigned to legal authorizations such as warrants or search warrants. In one instance, the investigator assigned was dyslexic and saw 4's as 7's and vice versa.

Example: Misidentification of a suspect resulting in wrongful detention.

Example: The efforts of a prolonged undercover investigation were wasted when through the poor judgment by the undercover investigator, he was recognized and identified.

There are many who hold the theory that good investigators are born, not made. Others hold that training and experience can produce a competent investigator. It is our belief that all of these are true with one additional attribute—COMMON SENSE!

A successful investigation is one in which:

- A logical sequence is followed.
- All available physical evidence is legally obtained.
- All witnesses are effectively interviewed.
- All suspects are legally and effectively interrogated.
- All leads are thoroughly developed.
- All details of the case are accurately and completely recorded and reported.

80

Investigating Fuel Theft

Both public and private investigators are at times required to investigate the theft of fuel(s), particularly gasoline. This can best be accomplished to the satisfaction of either civil or criminal prosecutions or suits by adding a foreign substance to the fuel/gasoline (one that will not interfere with the operation of a motor or engine). It must be invisible to the naked eye, inexpensive, and easily detected even if the fuel substance is diluted by the addition of untreated fuel. The technique described in this section is attributed to the Enforcement Law and Criminal Investigation for U.S. Treasury Agents.

The necessary material(s) include a 5 percent solution of sodium carbonate. This is available in chemical supply houses, drug stores, and academic and professional laboratories. Never use sodium hydroxide or sodium bicarbonate. A one-half gallon clear container with a sealing cap is also required. An amount of phenolphthalein (not phednolphthalin) is also required, the amount is determined by the amount of fuel/gasoline to be treated for identification purposes. For example, one ounce will treat 10,000 gallons of fuel/gasoline. This substance is relatively inexpensive and readily available.

The following steps must be implemented if the fuel/gasoline is to be identified and traced. First, test the untreated identified fuel/gasoline by placing 3 pints/1 1/2 quarts of untreated gasoline in the half-gallon bottle. Add 1/2 ounce of sodium carbonate solution. Secure the bottle and vigorously shake the bottle for at least two minutes. Invert the bottle and examine the water layer on the bottom. The water must remain clear and colorless. Empty the bottle and thoroughly wash it.

Second, identify or tag the fuel/gasoline by placing one ounce of phenolphthalein for each 10,000 gallons of fuel in a clear quart bottle. Fill the bottle about three fourths full of alcohol. Seal and shake until the phenolphthalein is dissolved. The contents of the bottle are sufficient to tag or identify 10,000 gallons of fuel/gasoline. It is best to add this solution to the substance to be identified as it is being pumped into the storage tank and also better if it is added in small doses. Obviously, if the storage tank is smaller, say 5,000 gallons, then add one half of the contents of the solution. Caution should be taken to make sure that fuel/gas in the pipeline has been cleaned out so that only the tagged or identified fuel/gasoline is available.

To test for the unauthorized distribution of or possession of any tagged fuel/gasoline, the following steps should be followed:

- Place approximately 2 pints or 1 quart of the suspect fuel/gasoline in a half gallon bottle.
- Add one-half ounce of sodium carbonate solution. Seal the sample and shake vigorously for at least two minutes.
- Invert the bottle and examine the water layer at the bottom. It should be a bluish pink.

81
Investigating International Cargo Theft

The investigation of losses of cargo in international commerce begins with the understanding that the sources of information and intelligence are determined by the mode of transportation used or the combination thereof. The sources may include the following:

- Shippers
- Manufacturers

- Consignees
- Intermodel transporters
- Warehouses
- Container freight stations or break bulk facilities
- Freight handlers, including forklift and crane operators, lorrie movers, and internal cargo movers
- Insurance companies
- Importers/exporters/Customs brokers
- U.S. Customs Service
- Federal Bureau of Investigation
- Federal Maritime Commission
- U.S. Department of Labor
- Internal Revenue Service
- U.S. Department of Transportation
- State/local law enforcement agencies. This includes air and seaport police, burglary, intelligence/organized crime units, and others as appropriate. Several departments have established specific squads to address the problem (i.e., Los Angeles and Miami).
- Foreign governments agencies and appropriate authorities from origin countries
- Appropriate councils, organizations, associations: for example, American Trucking Association, Air Transport Association, Waterfront Commission of New York Harbor, Association of Marine Underwriters, international associations, sea and airport police, and the National Cargo Security Council

82

Investigation Basics

Without an investigation, any knowledge of or observation of a crime or violation of law(s) (or in the case of corporations, policy and procedures) renders any suspicions or deductions useless. Any reports, memos, statements, formal or informal complaints require a response of some form of action. The initial report may come from victims, witnesses, responsible charge persons, and those responsible for the discovery of the violation or crime.

Personal traits a good investigator must have are:

- A high degree of initiative; the ability to see what has to be done and then do it
- Perseverance and "sticktoitiveness"
- Capacity to think through situations clearly
- Understanding of people
- Never underestimates or takes for granted anything
- Is not judgmental
- Curious mind and a strong desire to learn
- High degree of integrity and honesty
- Never seeks publicity or steals credit for the effort of others; gives credit where it is due and acknowledges the efforts of others

The age-old six elements in conducting an investigation should be the guide: WHO, WHAT, WHERE, WHEN, HOW and WHY. Getting the answers to all of these will most likely solve the specific crime or violation or at least provide a good start. Remember to use the five senses of sight, hearing, touch, smell, and taste.

It is imperative that you record and document your efforts. It is not always possible to carry around a laptop or digital camera, so note taking remains the basis for a report. After 24 hours, the average person will only remember approximately 85 percent of what he or she has done. Therefore, your notes should be accurate, understandable, legible, have all the facts, and contain accurate measurements and number notations if applicable.

In addition to photographs when appropriate, be they digital or regular, it is also wise to make sketches. These can be a back up to any photographs, but more importantly, they will assist the investigator in his or her recall of specifics such as where items were found, layout, direction, condition, and any other details it is important for the investigator to recall. Remember, all photos and sketches must be supported by investigative notes in order to be believable or credible.

83

Investigation Technology

The differences between the technology of twenty years ago and today are astonishing. Consider the use of a Polaroid camera to a 35 mm camera and now digital imaging. Taking photos at a crime scene has always been important in order to record evidence and for use in court. Now a digital camera captures the crime scene (remotely even) and then transmits the findings to a forensic lab.

In the next couple of years, we will see more and more high tech product become available. This will be followed by standards governing its uses and abuses. Following is a brief list of new technology:

1. Kodak has created the capability to make presentations electronically in a courtroom
2. Ground penetration radar is being used to detect and find buried bodies
3. Virtual reality and 3-D viewing of crime scenes
4. Biometrics
5. Retinal scans and facial imaging including simulation
6. Handwriting and voice analysis
7. Computerized patterning
8. Atmospheric iodine sampling (DOE) used to help detect a meth lab
9. Satellite technology and magnification
10. GPS tracking devices

84

Investigative Interviewing, The Art of[60]

PRINCIPLES OF QUESTION FORMULATION

The following guidelines will help you formulate effective interview questions:

- Avoid third-degree questioning.
- Use closed questions when appropriate.
- Use open questions when appropriate.
- Keep your questions simple.
- Avoid asking questions with more than one meaning.
- Dare to ask tough questions.
- Assume a positive response.
- Using leading questions when attempting to assist the interviewee to rationalize or save face.
- Ask self-appraisal questions; for example, "Has there been any time when you have thought of stealing from the company, even though you never actually did?"
- Handle trial-balloon questions cautiously.
- Assume that more information is available.

85

Investigative Interviewing: Types of Questions[61]

Knowing how to use various questions is like knowing how to use special codes that unlock a storehouse of information: in this case, the memory of the interviewee. This section explores the types of questions that can reveal your interest in the interviewee and the matter under investigation, express empathy, and promote human interaction. With a broader look at the types of questions, you will become better equipped to discover information.

Two main types of questions are generally asked during investigative interviews:

1. Closed questions usually require a simple yes or no answer, or an undeniable fact such as name, address, and so on. Use this type at the beginning of interviews ("The Initial Phase") to encourage affirmative responses and to put interviewees more at ease. Later in the interview, closed questions hamper your effort to discover information.
2. Open questions begin with a stated or implied who, where, what, when, how, and why and cannot be answered with a simple yes or no. They require the interviewee to think clearly, and although they can trigger the most distress in the interviewee, they also reveal the greatest amount of information.

86

Investigative Interviewing: Closed Questions[62]

Closed questions require only a simple answer. Examples include yes or no questions and multiple-choice questions. They are useful when you want to maintain maximum control over the interview and save time, because they limit the interviewee's response options. They are also used with reluctant interviewees who are not expected to give detailed explanations. Closed questions have the advantage of eliciting details, but they can inhibit the development of rapport. They are misused if the interviewer uses closed questions for detailed probing before the interviewee is ready. People will be willing to provide details, particularly about sensitive subjects, only if they feel comfortable.

87

Investigative Interviewing: Open Questions[63]

Open questions help interviews flow by tapping an interviewee's objective and subjective thinking. The investigator may ask the sample questions, "Why would anyone think you had something to do with the loss? Is there something that you have said or done that would have provoked suspicion?" With these questions, you are asking the interviewee to reflect on real events and their appearances. The innocent may say, "Well, I did pay off several bills just after the loss, but I got that money from my uncle." The guilty may say, "Well, I, ah, no, not that I can think of," even though this interviewee took an expensive vacation and bought a new car soon after the theft. Why didn't the interviewee mention the car and vacation?

A question beginning with "Why" is a particularly tricky question because it can sound challenging. It asks the interviewee to think, and furthermore, to reveal those private thoughts. Revelation leaves the interviewee open to judgment. You need to learn the cause, reason, or purpose, but the interviewee's answer may leave him or her open to rejection and misunderstanding. An interviewee may withdraw into silence or prevaricate. Anticipate the impact of each question you use, and be careful in formulating them. Open questions can help you:

- Discover the interviewee's priorities, attitudes, needs, values, and aspirations
- Determine the interviewee's frame of reference, and assist in establishing empathic understanding
- Build and enhance rapport
- Engage in active listening, stroking, and positive regard
- Allow and encourage the interviewee to express feelings and facts without feeling threatened
- Promote catharsis or express of the interviewee's emotions

There are a variety of types of open questions, each with its own character-istics and use. Reflective, directive, pointed, indirect, self-appraisal, diversion, and leading questions are discussed below. Kept sharp and ready through practice, these questions do more than probe—they set the stage for subsequent questions.

88

Investigative Interviewing: Types of Open Questions[64]

REFLECTIVE QUESTIONS

Reflective questions are like mirrors reflecting the interviewee's comments. They are used to handle objections from the interviewee, and often take the form of, "Let me see if I've got this straight . . ." or, "What I hear you say, then, is that you prefer not to comment about what you know because you don't want what you say to get back to Bob, is that right? Well, let me assure you that what we talk about is confidential and I won't tell Bob about our talk." Having said this, repeat the question that triggered the interviewee's objection. By removing the obstacle to cooperation, you assist the interviewee to feel more comfortable responding to your subsequent questions.

DIRECTIVE QUESTIONS

Directive questions are used to direct the interviewee's attention to areas of common ground with the investigator. Interviewees often need to hear the advantages of cooperation. They are in unknown territory with unknowable consequences, and a directive question answers this concern, as in: "You do want to get to the bottom of this, don't you? I would think you'd want your side of the story in the report so that no one misunderstands what happened," or, "I'm sure you don't want anyone to think you tried to hurt her, isn't that so?"

POINTED QUESTIONS

Pointed questions stir interviewees into action. They are specific in nature and design, pointing most precisely at the goal. Pointed questions are complex, detailed, and persuasive. Most of the questions asked in forensic interviews are pointed questions. By asking exactly what is you want to know, these questions show interviewees that you believe they are ready, willing, and able to respond. These questions, which are based on the self-fulfilling prophecy, work most of the time. Pointed questions need not be offensive or accusatory. On the contrary, they must be thoroughly developed and subtly applied to avoid provoking stress and defensiveness in the interviewee. You can gently stimulate the interviewee's thinking with pointed, creative questions. For example, if you believe that the interviewee accidentally set a fire, you might ask, "On the day of the fire, how often did you smoke in the storeroom?"

INDIRECT QUESTIONS

Pointed questions are not always appropriate. Indirect questions are sometimes more successful because they help interviewees save face and rationalize their behavior. Indirect questions allow the interviewee to express his or her opinions, suggestions, feelings, and so on. They give the interviewee a sense of permission by taking the form, "I've talked to many of the other employees, and they believe that.... Do you agree?" Indirect questions help you understand the interviewee's thoughts, needs and values. Questions of this type are often used at the beginning of an interview and as a change of pace during the course of the discussion. They can also be used as diversion questions (see the following section on diversion questions).

SELF-APPRAISAL QUESTIONS

Self-appraisal questions are used to stimulate conversation, encourage the interviewee to identify with the delinquent, and reveal truthfulness or deception. These questions might take the following form: "If you are faced with a lot of pressures at home and you had all this temptation here at work with all of this money, what would prevent you from stealing?" or "Have you ever thought of stealing any money here, even though you never did?" or, "Is it possible you may have been seen in the area of the money, even for a brief time?" Self-appraisal questions help the investigator develop a hypothesis about how and why an incident took place and who may have been involved. When asking such questions, the investigator uses a floating-point strategy to find solid ground upon which to build a hypothesis. This hypothesis is confirmed or modified by interviewee responses that may reveal information, distress, or evasion.

That which is deeply rooted in your being determines your verbal and non-verbal responses. If I asked you if you think abortion is good or bad, your response will reflect your deeply rooted conviction. The circumstances, however, will influence the candor of your response. If you know that I am a strong advocate of abortion, but I am your friend or colleague, or even more powerfully, your supervisor, you will probably modify your comments to prevent revealing the strength of your position. This modification is extremely difficult to hide. To modify responses to self-appraisal questions, the interviewee first has to think of an answer, decide that the answer would not sound good, then make up a new story, and tell it convincingly. It is almost impossible for deceptive or evasive interviewees to be consistent in answering self-appraisal questions.

DIVERSION QUESTIONS

Diversion questions have two purposes: they distract the interviewee's thoughts from a tension-producing issue, and they build rapport between the investigator and the interviewer. To temporarily divert an interviewee's anger or fear may be extremely difficult because the strength of that anger or fear is so strong that clear thinking is all but eliminated. Diversion questions are useful when dealing with highly emotional interviewees. Their use delays the inquiry into the specific nature of the incident until the interviewee has regained his or her composure.

As an illustration, when talking with a customer that witnessed a bank robbery, it was evident that she was shaken by her experience. She needed time to realize that the danger was over. Therefore, I spoke with firm reassurance that all was safe. I tried to break her focus on the fear caused by the robbery and help her think clearly about what she saw. Initially in a state of shock, her thinking hazy, she gradually began to sense that she could relax. My diversion questions dealt with topics unrelated to the robbery, questions she could answer with ease, such as, "What type of work do you do Mary?" and "Have you lived in this community many years?" Gradually she became able to focus her thoughts on what she saw and heard during the robbery.

Diversion questions often focus on someone or something more important and attractive to the interviewee than the incident under investigation. I was called in by a business owner to investigate a burglary that had been reported to the local police. The incident involved the theft of about $3,000 from a retail business. The money had been stored in a file cabinet. The details of the crime are not, now, as critical as explaining the police response and the owner's angry reaction to that response. The first, and only, police officer at the crime scene told the owner that, in all probability, no fingerprints had been left at the crime scene. No detective arrived to search for evidence or conduct interviews. The case was administratively closed, all of which infuriated the owner.

The main point here is that the owner, in the process of providing me with preliminary information, was preoccupied with the "bad job" done by the police rather than the details that might help me fulfill my obligations. To refocus the owner's anger, I diverted attention from the crime in an attempt to quell that anger and disappointment. I said something like, "You certainly have a beautiful place here, it looks like you people take pride in their work!" He responded, and I said, "It must have taken many years to reach this point of development. How long have you been in business?" I tried not to appear lacking in empathy, or make my diversions too obvious or too abrupt, but rather connected to the inquiry. I wanted the interviewee to intentionally switch off the emotion about the police and begin thinking clearly about the details of the crime.

Diversion questions may help you to develop and strengthen rapport when you use them to indicate that you have investigated similar matters with similar interviewees. When I announce that many victims feel violated and confused, the interviewee realizes that I have insight into the feelings of victims. In one of my investigations in which a woman received sexually explicit letters, she wondered what she had done to cause the man to send the letters. "How did I lead him on?" she wondered out loud. I tried to reassure her that she was probably at the wrong place at the wrong time and she didn't do anything to deserve or provoke those letters. Diversion questions usually help diffuse a tense situation.

LEADING QUESTIONS

Leading questions include some assumption on the part of the investigator. For example, the statement "From what you say, you must have had a rough time in that job last summer" contains an assumption and invites the interviewee to elaborate or explain. Leading questions containing implicit messages can be used to maintain a moderate emotional tension in the interviewee, but they need not be abrasive if thoughtfully constructed, as in, "You're under a lot of strain at home, aren't you?" or "You're not the kind of person who would use that missing money for drugs, are you?" Leading questions are usually thought to produce invalid, unreliable answers. This is true when they are poorly used. However, when they are used to build rapport and communicate your understanding and acceptance, leading questions stimulate dialogue and encourage cooperation. They exhibit your assumption that the interviewee can and will provide truthful information.

89

Investigative Interviewing: Question Filter Factors[65]

Throughout your career, you will learn to use certain tactics when gathering information during an interview. For example, you will learn to build rapport with the interviewee, to maintain a positive attitude, and to listen actively. These tactics, which I call "filter factors" will—if used sensitively and skillfully—have significant and positive effects on the outcome of your interviews. I call them filter factors because they help the interviewer display favorable characteristics and screen out less favorable ones. They are designed to show the interviewee that the interviewer can be trusted. In most interviews, the investigator has at least one hidden agenda, some unannounced reason for conducting the interview. For example, one hidden agenda when interviewing a victim is to determine if a crime actually took place. While the victim may think only that you are seeking details, at the same time you are watching for any signs of fabrication.

In one of my investigations, the female manager of a convenience store reported being taken by force in her van to a secluded part of town after she was surprised by a thief who had been hiding in the back of her van. The thief assaulted her as she drove to the bank one evening with about $3,000 of receipts from the store. She claimed the thief ordered her to drive to a parking area and forced her to walk with him down toward a lake where he told her to stand while he drove away in her van. But it had been snowing and there was only one pair of shoe prints in the snow. Confronted with the inconsistencies of her story, she confessed stealing the money to pay family bills. She had hidden portions of the stolen money in the rafters of her garage where police detectives found it.

Practiced use of the filter factors can help the interviewer keep the hidden agenda hidden. During the first few minutes of the interview, begin using the filter factors that follow and continue using them during the primary phase and even into the follow-up. These filter factors are:

- Consider the human needs of interview participants.
- Continue to build and maintain rapport.
- Apply flexible methods.
- Cover your suspicions.
- Use creative imagination.
- Apply the self-fulfilling prophecy.
- Exhibit human warmth, sensitivity, empathy, respect, and genuineness.

- Use nonjudgmental acceptance
- Cover your personal values.
- Use active, attentive listening.
- Be patient.
- Be "positive." Use positive silence, positive eye contact, positive proximics, positive kinetics, and use positive haptics where appropriate.
- Maintain a positive, neutral stance.
- Maintain a positive attitude.
- Use positive power and positive control.
- Control personal anger—avoid antagonizing or harassing interviewees.
- Avoid using coercive behaviors.
- Use observation, evaluation, and assessment.
- Avoid using the third degree.
- Use closed questions and open questions when appropriate.
- Keep your questions simple and avoid using questions with double meanings.
- Dare to ask tough questions.
- Use unasked questions (assume the answer is yes).
- Properly use leading questions, and use self-appraisal questions.
- Handle trial-balloon questions.
- Finally, always assume that more data is available.

90

Investigative Interviewing: Tactics When Seeking a Confession[66]

It is vital to avoid saying or doing anything that might cause an innocent person to confess. Be fair and practical when interrogating anyone, particularly a suspect in custody. Consider the following legal tactics in an interrogation:

- Exhibit your confident judgment that the subject committed, or shared in committing, the crime.

- Present any circumstantial evidence to buttress your judgment and persuade the subject that denial is useless.
- Watch the subject's behavior for indications of lying.
- Empathize with and help the subject rationalize his or her participation and save face when talking about it.
- Minimize the significance of the matter under investigation.
- Offer nonjudgmental acceptance of the subject's behavior.
- Encourage the subject to tell the truth.

91

Investigative Interviewing: Trickery[67]

Trickery and deceit are often used in interrogations. The Supreme Court has given tacit recognition to the necessity of these tactics. In 1969, the Court held: "The fact that the police misrepresented the statements that [a suspected accomplice] had made is, while relevant, insufficient in our view to make this otherwise voluntary confession inadmissible. These cases must be decided by viewing the totality of the circumstances."

92

The Investigative Process[68]

An *investigation* is the examination, study, search for, tracking, and gathering of factual information that answers questions or solves problems. It is more of an art than a science. Although the person engaged in investigation is a gatherer of facts, he or she must develop hypotheses and draw conclusions based on available information. The investigative process, then, is a comprehensive activity involving information collection, the application of logic, and the exercise of sound reasoning. The end result of an investigation is the factual explanation of what transpired if the incident or issue is over, or of what is occurring if the issue is of the present.

The investigative process is not limited to the criminal justice and security fields. It is an activity found, to one extent or another, in virtually all areas of human endeavor. Academicians are investigators, supervisors faced with disciplinary problems are investigators, medical doctors are investigators, just to name a few. Sherlock Holmes with deerstalker hat and magnifying glass may be the art's most familiar image, but investigation does not belong exclusively to the realm of cops and robbers.

Just as the art of investigation belongs to no one province, so no one has all the answers as to precisely how any investigation can led to the desired solution. Too many facets are involved in the process of information collection, the application of logic, and sound reasoning. Some such facets include intuition, luck, mistakes, and the often touted "gut feeling." No single textbook of formulas is possible; no one book (or author) can stand alone as the ultimate authority. Our purpose, then, is an overview of investigative concepts, strategies, suggestions, guidelines, hints, and examples that can be useful to any investigator.

There are two categories of investigation: constructive and reconstructive. *Constructive investigations* are covert in nature, performed in secrecy. This type of inquiry occurs while the suspected activity is taking place or anticipated. An example might be an investigation into a complaint that a member of middle management solicits sexual favors from female subordinates and reaps favors accordingly. The purpose of the constructive investigation is to determine if objectionable activity is taking place. *Reconstructive investigations* are necessary when an event has taken place and the investigator must recreate what happened after the fact. This type of investigation is usually overt in nature, carried out in the open.

THE INVESTIGATIVE PROCESS

As it pertains to the security industry, the investigative process is organizationally oriented as opposed to being community oriented. Its objective in this setting is to seek answers to the basic questions—the what, who, where, when, how and why—regarding a condition, incident, or action deemed organizationally unacceptable, or to meet organizational objectives. Internal dishonesty, for example, is an organizationally unacceptable activity. The background investigation of a prospective new employee would meet one organizational objective.

Most of the investigative process takes place in the collection of information. This gathering or collection is based on *communication* and *observation*. The answers to the six basic investigative questions will be developed through communication—that is, the written or spoken word—or by observation—that is, physical evidence that can be observed (whether by human eye or microscope), touched, or in any way quantitatively measured.

93

Investigative Reports: Effective Construction

An eighteenth-century scientist named Pascal writing to a friend said, "I hope you will pardon me for writing such a long letter, but I did not have the time to write a shorter one." Take the time to make sure your investigative work has clarity and conciseness. There are four items that will help to achieve this: punctuation, arrangement, sentence length, and paragraph length.

PUNCTUATION

If you keep your writing short and simple, then your sentences need little or no punctuation. You use punctuation to give clarity in meaning. The comma is the most misused of all punctuation marks. A simple rule is, when in doubt, leave it out. There is also a tendency to overuse semicolons. Overuse of the semicolon leads to involved sentences that are difficult to understand. More often than not, you can simply make a new sentence. Really good writing can be readily understood with a minimum of punctuation.

ARRANGEMENT

Proper arrangement is attained through practice, plus some forethought before you begin writing the report. Use the outline method guided by the tried and true answers to who, what, where, when, how, and why.

SENTENCE LENGTH

How long should be sentence be? In Queen Elizabeth's day the average written sentence was about 45 words. Many have stated that the level of writing as found in the *Reader's Digest* is the current standard; these sentences average 17 words. It is important to be guided by the fact that short sentences avoid the pitfalls of grammar and punctuation, but too much starting and stopping makes for unpleasant reading.

PARAGRAPHS

A *paragraph* is a group of sentences that relate one to another. The paragraph is not a unit of length but a unit of thought. Never ask a reader to group too much without a break. You must never assemble in one paragraph sentences that do not have unity of thought. A paragraph should be a complete development of a topic. You can probably say all you need to in a paragraph of about 150 words. You should not exceed 300 words.

Above all, avoid gobbledygook!!!

94

Investigative Reports: Preparation

The results of any efforts by an investigator conclude in some form of a text report. Of course, the specific purpose of an investigative report is to present all the pertinent data and/or facts relating to a matter in order for appropriate action and decisions to be made. This is the same for both public and private investigators. Your goal in formulating your report is to communicate information so that any readers or reviewers clearly understand the data presented. To have value, the report must be written so that any reader comprehends the full significance of its contents. Furthermore, they should be convinced of the thoroughness of the investigative actions taken and willing to act based on the data presented.

When preparing the investigative data, you must make every effort to preclude the reader or reviewer from drawing erroneous conclusions or inferences. You are not writing fiction and do not have the advantage of facial expressions, tone of voice or gestures. A good rule of thumb is to always put yourself in the place of the reader or reviewer.

The standards to follow are simple, and if followed can guarantee desired results for your investigative efforts. The standards are:

- Write to express and not to impress.
- Use terms and words familiar to the reader or reviewer.
- Don't simply record facts, but also communicate your findings.
- Keep your audience in mind and tie your delivery to their level of experience.

Remember that what you end up with is a permanent record of evidence obtained by investigative efforts. What you have is a history to refresh your memory. Remember to be fair in what you are reporting. Do not distort the significance of the facts and data. Report your findings so that they speak for themselves. When quoting comments, do so exactly. Never stress rumor or gossip. Remember to be politically correct in your expression and do not make offensive remarks about race, religion, or sexual persuasion. The exception to this is when quoting directly.

Remember to be unemotional, unbiased, and impartial. Do not exaggerate and never let your conclusions surpass the facts you have gathered. Opinions, conclusions, and inferences may be helpful but you must identify them as such. Any conclusions stated in a report should be based on facts previously set forth.

95

Investigative Reports: Standards for Writing

The basic standards are that you be clear and concise. This can be achieved by omitting unnecessary words. Simply put, don't be verbose.

Prefer single words to circumlocution: "knows" instead of "fully cognizant of."

Prefer the familiar to the supposedly learned: "begin" instead of "initiate" or "commence."

Prefer the concrete word to the abstract: abstract—"we found a large quantity of stolen appliances"; concrete—"we found a total of nine stolen appliances."

Prefer the short word to the long. Examples are:

A *true fact* vs. a *fact*
All leaders vs. *leader*
Are clearly indicated vs. *are seen*
Are desirous of vs. *want to*
At all times vs. *always*
Red in color vs. *red*

Use the active voice when you wish to promote emphasis and conciseness: active—"He gave me an invoice"; passive—"An invoice was given to me by him." Always use the active voice when the doer of the action is more important than the recipient. Use the passive when the recipient is more important. For example, in "A course in report writing was given at the school," the recipient (course) is more important than the doer (whoever gave the course).

A successful investigative report must have a logical presentation. Everything in the report should be relevant to a main idea. It must have unity. Use topic headings where necessary for major parts of the report. The topic heading should succinctly describe what follows. Each paragraph under the heading should have a unit of thought germane to that heading.

I recommend five standard steps in preparing a report. These steps are:

1. Outline
2. Organize the available material (notes, statements, documents, printouts/records, exhibits)
3. Write
4. Edit and evaluate
5. Revise/rewrite

96

Investigative Tips on Fax Fraud

With "road warriors" making good use of every available moment when traveling on the road and faxing data, reports, and other company confidential material back to their offices or other concerned parties, there are many opportunities for the interception of transmission(s). You must accept that on the contra roll in the fax apparatus you might choose to use from an airport, business center, or hotel, there will be a readable copy of your message. More obviously, the operator may make a copy of your fax transmission or of a fax sent to you.

There is an extra danger if you are staying in a hotel arranged or recommended and perhaps paid for by a business partner or client. It is not difficult to arrange for artful monitoring of an unsuspecting business traveler. There is also a potential for persons unknown or unauthorized to gain access to your machine and give the impression to an unsuspecting business that they are dealing directly with your firm-authorized representatives.

Since it is possible to deprogram the origin or sender identification along with date, time, and recipient information, for control purposes you should require legitimate/authorized fax transmissions to have such data on the cover sheet. This will aid an investigation if it becomes necessary and will ensure that all your faxes were sent and received at the right time and in order.

Certain types of white collar fraud/crime are more readily adaptable to fax misuse. Among them, diversion is high on the list. Uplifted "corrections" to shipments of goods is but example.

Fax cover sheets are duplicated as needed, and laptop computers store a fax transmission format. Neither of these is usually numbered or coded in any manner for control purposes; doing so, along with fax logs, can do much to deter misuse and fraud.

NOTE: Some of the material research for proof of incidents first appeared in *Hoffman's Detective's Tips For Business and Industry*, Volume 54, Amsterdam, Holland: Hoffman Investigation Ltd. Publications.

97

Investigations: 50 Things You Should Know[69]

The following items are key points that you should know when considering investigations of all types. These include investigations by both proprietary staff and private consultants and vendors.

1. The principal purpose for conducting a background investigation (BI) is to verify the truthfulness and accuracy of an applicant's statements.
2. The single most important tool for applicant information is the employment application.
3. Never hire or formally accept an applicant until a BI has been completed. If you have no choice, then temper your offer as contingent upon a successful BI.
4. Net worth and/or financial investigations should be implemented if an employee is a suspect of internal theft, or when they are employed in sensitive work for the company.
5. A lifestyle investigation is used to determine suitability for a specific position or continued employment.
6. Prior to offering promotion or transfer to an employee, a net worth investigation should be performed.
7. The process of interviewing during the course of an investigation of someone who is a suspect or refuses to completely disclose should be considered hostile.
8. Dangers associated with hostile interviewee/investigation include: violations of the Fair Trade Commission (FTC) Act or Fair Credit Reporting Act; Equal Employment Opportunity Complaints; unfair labor practices; or invasion of privacy.
9. The two main types of investigations are direct and indirect.
10. Statements and confessions must be voluntarily offered or given. No threats, promises, or coercion can be used.
11. Anyone giving a voluntary statement must be adequately and appropriately advised of their rights.
12. There are three types of statement: narrative, question and answer, or a combination of both.
13. There are three types of deception detection devices: voice analysis, the psychological stress evaluation (PSE), and the polygraph or lie detector.

14. Remember that the polygraph examination is only as good as the operator performing the service.
15. There are several types of incident that can be investigated: claims of fraud in workers' compensation, theft, misconduct, arson and related concerns, sabotage, industrial spying or espionage, and traffic accidents.
16. When collecting evidence, make sure to photograph and sketch the evidence prior to moving the articles of evidence.
17. When marking evidence in an investigation, make sure to mark the date and time and place a distinctive identifying mark of your own.
18. When preserving evidence, make sure to package it appropriately, transport or move it properly, maintain safety and security, and limit or restrict the chain of custody.
19. There are two types of surveillance: overt and covert.
20. There are three basic forms of surveillance: physical, technical with various forms of electronic or hardware devices, and documentary or paper trail.
21. In order for there to be a discharge for employee misconduct or theft, the evidence must be credible.
22. Rules associated with discharge must be reasonable, communicated to the employee, enforced with impartiality, and within the authority of management and supervision.
23. During investigative interviews, the employee has the right to have a union representative present if he or she suspects that some disciplinary action may take place.
24. The employer does not have to offer that the union representative be present. The employee must request one.
25. Any suspect employee has the right to be counseled by his or her union representative.
26. Your suspect must be proven guilty by the courts based on your investigation, report, and findings.
27. The Bureau of Vital Statistics can provide information on marriage licenses.
28. Nitrocellulose, dynamite, and detonation each are extremely dangerous and leave behind a specific piece of evidence.
29. Polygraph is a great tool but it depends a lot on the examiner.
30. Many polygraph tests are inconclusive and take about 15 minutes.
31. Consider the polygraph examiner a member of your investigation team.
32. Psychological stress analyzers are based on voice modulation and the individual's stress.
33. The Civil Rights Law of 1964 is important because it means:
    a. You can't question a suspect prior to his/her arrest.
    b. Job applications cannot inquire about prior arrests
    c. Job applications that contain blanks could lead to the applicant's rights being violated.
34. Interview the suspect with a bare minimum of distractions.
35. Experience and the ability to blend in are the key words in undercover work.
36. A key function for any investigator is to report all illegal activity.

37. Schizophrenic individuals have a mental disorder.
38. *Corpus delicti* is having a confession, but you need a body to prove your case.
39. *Entrapment* is leading a person to or inducing them to commit a crime.
40. *Venue* is the place where the crime took place.
41. The *exclusionary rule* is evidence illegally obtained.
42. The Fifth Amendment is on self-incrimination.
43. The Secret Service primarily deals with counterfeiting money.
44. Federal kidnapping kicks in after the victim is missing for 24 hours.
45. There are nine Justices who sit on the United States Supreme Court.
46. The Uniform Crime Report (UCR) is put out around October of each year by the U.S. Department of Justice.
47. A *battery* is the use of force against another; it requires touching.
48. A *subpoena* is a court order directing an individual to appear before it and testify.
49. OSHA regulations have been around since 1971.
50. *Arson* is the deliberate burning of the home or building of another.

98

Investigator Job Description: 32 Discrete Services[70]

1. Locating bugging apparatus
2. Identifying the writers of anonymous letters
3. Investigating the background of companies, job applicants, and prospective business partners
4. Proving fraud
5. Providing advice on business security (security surveys)
6. Tracing business espionage
7. Checking the activities of representatives, mechanics, and drivers
8. Proving and combating blackmail
9. Proving computer fraud/losses
10. Demonstrating infringements of competition conditions

11. Proving breach of contract
12. Investigating theft
13. Investigating fraud
14. Proving infringement of secrecy clauses
15. Due diligence inquiries
16. Proving breaches of patent rights/licenses
17. Investigating internal theft
18. Undertaking cash controls
19. Proving malversations
20. Proving misuse of goods and business data
21. Proving dishonest competition
22. Locating money, goods, and people
23. Providing personal security advice
24. Investigating sabotage
25. Investigating damage claims
26. Investigating bribery
27. Tracing leaks of business information
28. Proving embezzlement
29. Investigating swindles
30. Investigating corruption
31. Investigating absenteeism
32. Investigating other suspicious activity not listed

99

Investigators as Problem Solvers: A Complex Mixture of Many Simple Facts[71]

The old adage that knowledge is power is particularly emphasized when considering the potential impact of investigations. The investigative process differentiates between learning and misunderstanding. Investigations are often performed by people who are highly theoretical and philosophical but do not directly consider themselves theorists or philosophers.

Investigators are similar to social scientists in their necessity to utilize methodology. As investigators, we intuitively know that the problems for which we pursue solutions must first be defined. Without framing a definition, an investigator would simply waste resources and fit the wrong pieces into a puzzle. At the same token, investigations are sometimes closed by luck. One of the authors was an investigator in Chicago when he was walking down the street in the uptown area of the north side one afternoon when he literally bumped into a parolee for whom he had a murder warrant. The parolee simply gave up, but his companion wanted to fight. Both were arrested and booked. After booking, it was found that the companion was wanted for escaping from a federal prison. When contacted by an FBI agent and asked how this escapee, who had alluded authorities for fourteen months had been captured, the young investigator simply stated, "Solid police work." A promotion followed shortly thereafter.

Investigations are often not exciting. But criminal justice students and many patrolmen want to become investigators because the position either seems romantic or appears to be a better way to spend an eight-hour shift. In reality, investigations are very demanding because of having to make good use of one's time, knocking on the doors of people who would rather not be talking to you, getting called into court on odd days if other police happen to pick up your perpetrator, and even getting "rousted" by police in different parts of the city if you happen to be in a big city or in a different part of the state in which you are not known. The excitement comes after a lot of hard work, immediately prior to closing a case. Then the investigator realizes that there are other cases at various levels of closure requiring tedious attention within different phases of the investigator's methodological model.

Taking a college course does not make you an investigator, ready to pursue serial killers. Effective investigators are eclectic and interdisciplinary and use the knowledge at their fingertips, as well as creating knowledge. "Showoffs" do not make good investigators. By nature, investigators need to be "closed-mouthed" and patient until the information they seek is in. It is not possible to get all the information that you think you can get on a person you may be investigating. Moreover, information can, many times, come from areas you would never have guessed. The more you can accumulate information sources and particular information, the better investigator you will become over time because you will be consistently developing your methodology.

Becoming an investigator by rising through the ranks of a police agency has its benefits, since the officer has often developed some mannerisms that are effective in getting information from people. However, the opposite can also be true, if the officer cannot make the adjustment to managing time as an investigator. In the real world, an effective investigator has to be a salesman and marketer, have patience, learn how to walk and talk slower than usual, know how to think on his or her feet, be aware of where he or she is at when "working the street," and develop "networks" not only with the public on the streets, but also within your own department and at various levels of organizational and socioeconomic status. It is much better for an investigator not to develop an attitude of superiority, but to make contacts with those to whom you can regularly return.

Learning how to write is most important to enable defining the problem, explaining use of resources, and showing how you followed training procedures properly.

If a person is serious about becoming an investigator, another area that must be considered is family and time management. Regardless of how one gets into investigations, timing is always a factor in making a case. Timing is never based on luck, but comes from devotion to the job. Making time for the job by giving up other activities is common, but, unfortunately, often family related.

The rewards from the investigative profession can be owning your own company or having the flexibility to work varied hours, depending on the cases taken. Again, successful investigators spend tremendous amounts of time developing their contacts, either as police officers/investigators or civilian investigators, and they have learned to manage themselves, their caseloads and their free time, since "burnout" is easy to develop if motivation is wanting. And if motivation is wanting, poor investigations will follow since "half-truths" do not take as much effort as eliciting the whole truth. Investigators do not "predict," investigators "anticipate."

Investigators are not journalists and interviews are not just conversations between people having the same vested interests in the investigation's end result. When the investigator's report is filed, the outcome of the case may be positive or negative, used by competent or incompetent attorneys and/or clients, help or hurt the right or wrong people, or not even be considered. Also, courtroom cross-examination is not a casual interlude where only uncontrolled facts need to be put to a jury. It is mandatory that investigators learn some of the methods of other courtroom players to understand the true meaning of "land mine."

The investigator is neither judge and jury nor the one leading a charge to vindicate the accused or reward the victimized. But the investigator can have a tremendous impact on the process of the eventual outcome if his work is accurate or inaccurate, truthful or untruthful. The question to consider is this: how ethical and how accurate would you like or expect all concerned professionals to be in their input of making good management decisions or good law?

100

Liability for Investigators

As we were putting this book together, ASIS was conducting a workshop entitled "Liability for Investigations." Their course identified 13 points, which we have listed below for your review. For additional information about this course we suggest you contact ASIS for the date and time of their next program. Specific additional detail may be obtained from the ASIS Library O.P. Norton Information Resources Center, Internet address www.infoinc.com/product.html. In addition, ASIS offers an Advanced Investigation Program Workshop annually.

- Liability when conducting applicant background checks
- Liability for not conducting applicant background checks
- Detention and interrogation of employees
- Search and seizure in the workplace
- Undercover and surveillance operations
- Employee discharge and failure to discharge
- Discharge of employees for off-duty criminal conduct
- Disclosure of evidence in worker's compensation and unemployment hearings
- Release of adverse employee information
- Misrepresentation and failure to warn about ex-employees
- Filing of criminal charges
- Discrimination-based investigations
- Union and nonunion member investigations

101

"Lucky" Investigations

Over the years, we both have been involved in numerous investigations. Being lucky during an investigation is something we feel needs to be acknowledged. Fred Mullins, CPP, was telling us about a stakeout he was on. Five hours at a specific site and nothing. It was 5:00 AM and he decided to head home and go to bed. While traveling toward home on a major highway, the truck and the individuals he had been waiting for passed him on the left. Fred said, "I was lucky."

But was it luck, or being in the right place at the right time? What it dedication to the assignment? Was it knowing when to leave a stakeout? Was it a skilled investigator's hunch? Was it a degree of skill and a mixture of all of the above? We do know he completed his assignments and the individuals were arrested.

102

Mail Covers: An Investigative Tool

A mail cover is used to record information on the outside container, envelope, or wrapper of mail, including the name and address of the sender and the place and date of postmarking. Obtaining information from the cover of a piece of mail from the Postal Inspector or any other postal employee, without an authorized mail cover, is illegal and can jeopardize a case that goes to court.

Mail covers may be authorized only in criminal cases where information is needed to locate a fugitive or to obtain evidence of the commission or attempted commission of any crime punishable by imprisonment for a term of more than one year (felony). The mail cover is not an exploratory act and should not be requested as the initial step in any investigation. A mail cover request must be sent in writing to the Operations Support Group (OSG) that covers your area for the Postal Inspectors.

Where an emergency exists, the Postal Inspector in charge or designee may grant a mail cover based on an oral request. While the mail cover data will be released immediately, the requesting agency must submit a written request for the mail cover within three business days to the appropriate OSG.

A mail cover request must contain the following:

- Reason the mail is needed to locate a fugitive or to obtain information regarding the commission or the attempted commission of a felony
- Full name and complete address of the subject
- Classes of mail to be covered, including reasons for any class other than first-class
- How long the mail cover is to be in effect; mail covers are usually authorized for 30 days and extensions are available
- Laws suspected of being violated, including legal citations and penalties
- Whether the subject has been indicted and whether the subject has an attorney; if so, the attorney's name and address must be included
- How often the mail cover data is needed (daily, weekly, or less frequently)
- Additional circumstances relevant to the investigation. Information from a mail cover provides valuable investigative leads. The initial information itself is not evidence, and you should not refer to the use.

103

Management Cost Analysis Considerations of Theft Response

When confronted with a solution to employee theft, management must consider its options. The simple fact is that there are only two options: doing something or doing nothing. What is the cost of doing something versus doing nothing?

Conduct that damages an organization through actual losses due to theft or inappropriate behavior requires some positive corrective action for unacceptable events.

In this cost analysis model there are three areas to consider for the actions chosen to address a specific event. These are: psychological, social, and financial or economic. The idea for this model as shown in the chart must be credited to a survey developed in a project conducted by the Criminology Department, ERASMUS University, Rotterdam as supervised by Mr. J.C. Hess. It appeared first in the Hoffman Investigations Ltd. Publication, *Detectives' Tips for Business and Industry.*

	Cost of Doing Nothing	*Cost of Doing Something*
Psychological:	Breakdown of authority	Embarrassment for organization
	Prestige impact on personnel	Reaction of other employees
Social:	Negative influence on workforce	Influence can cause unrest
	Damage to organization's image	Publicity may cause client concern
Financial:	Creates a precedent	Actual disruption and loss
	Condones acceptance of loss	Cost of replacement, legal, and human resources

This study recognizes the reluctance of management for criminal action by reporting incidents to public enforcement authorities due to the fear of internal agitation, negative image, client reaction, and actual costs, including time and energy. It is logical with this thinking then for management to weigh the costs of doing nothing as opposed to doing something.

104

Miranda Warning[72]

Those who have police powers and the authority to make an arrest must give the Miranda warning to those individuals they have arrested, detained, and/or are questioning. Generally speaking, a Miranda warning may not be necessary from a security officer.

The following is the Miranda warning:

1. You have the right to remain silent.
2. Anything you say may be used against you.
3. You have the right to contact an attorney.
4. If you cannot afford an attorney, one will be provided free.
5. Do you understand these rights as I have given them to you?

105

Missing Children[73]

What has been referred to as the missing child problem is, in reality, at least five very different, distinct problems:

* Family abduction: Child taken in violation of custody agreement or decree
* Nonfamily abduction: The coerced and unauthorized taking of a child
* Runaways: Child left home without permission and stayed away.
* Throwaways: Any situation in which a child is told to leave home: a child left home and the parents refused to allow the child back; a child ran away and the parents took no action to recover the child; or a child was abandoned
* Lost, injured, or otherwise missing: Children missing because of miscommunication with caretakers, or because of disability or injury

The previous definitions are paraphrased from the Office of Juvenile Justice's research report entitled *Missing, Abducted, Runaway, and Throwaway Children in America.* The researchers recommended that public policy clarify its domain, and clearly differentiate each of the social problems under the "missing children" umbrella.

Federal legislation addressing the problem of missing children is The Uniform Child Custody Jurisdiction Act, which is a uniform law enacted between 1969 and 1983, with some variation, in all states and the District of Columbia. This law is a jurisdictional statute that addresses when a court has subject matter jurisdiction in a custody case: for example, which state is a child's "home state."

The telephone number for the National Center for Missing and Exploited Children is (800) THE LOST or (800) 843-5678. For more information, see the following section on Web sites for missing children.

106

Missing Children Web Sites[74]

Thousands of children are reported missing every year and agencies are turning to the Internet to help find them. Here are a few Web sites that offer listings of missing children (provided by Jeff Lowenthal).

National Center for Missing and Exploited Children (http://www.missingkids.org/): This organization has been involved with 50,000 cases and was instrumental in Beau's return to his mother. Its Web site receives 30,000 hits per week.

Child Quest International, Inc. (http://www.childquest.org): This site also includes listings of abductors for whom warrants have been issued.

The Polly Klaas Foundation (http://www.pollyklaas.org/): This foundation was originally formed to aid in the search of 12-year-old Polly Klaas, who was kidnapped and murdered. In addition to its listing of missing children, it has advice for parents and a downloadable child ID kit.

107

Modus Operandi[75]

Modus operandi (MO) is Latin for method of operation. An investigator may ask, "What was the method used by the burglar?" Because people differ, they commit crimes in different ways. Many police departments have MO files on offenders. When a crime takes place, investigators may check the MO files for suspects who are known to commit crimes in a certain way. A particular offender may use a specific tool during a burglary. A robber may wear a unique style of clothing during robberies. A saboteur at a manufacturing plant may be using a particular type of wire cutter. Sometimes, an uncommon MO is discovered: for example, a burglar who defecates at the crime scene.

108

Money Laundering and Postal Inspection

Money laundering is the process of altering the form, appearance, location, origin, source, ownership, or control of taxable income or of proceeds generated by an illegal activity. It is accomplished by one or more financial transactions whose purpose is to conceal the income or proceeds from the government.

Illegally obtained funds are generated through activities like drug trafficking, mail fraud, and embezzlement by a bank employee. Typically, "dirty" funds are transferred through one or more bank accounts or transactions, including those where postal money orders are purchased in the laundering process. Ultimately, the funds emerge as untraceable, "clean," legitimate-looking assets, such as money market deposits, real estate investments, or business ownership interests.

The Postal Inspection Service is one of several federal agencies with authority to investigate certain illegal activities that typically generate a large amount of cash which is laundered to conceal its true character. Among these agencies are the Internal Revenue Service, the Drug Enforcement Agency, and the Customs Service.

In order to better trace laundered funds, 18 USC 5325 requires that any financial institution that issues a bank check, money order, cashier's check, or traveler's check to any person must collect certain information from that person if the transaction is made in United States coins or currency in an amount greater than $3,000. This includes deposits, withdrawals, currency exchanges, or other payments or transfers by, through, or to the financial institution, unless the individual has a transaction account with the institution and certain efforts are made to identify the person making the transaction.

Multiple transactions must be treated by the financial institution as a single transaction if the institution knows these transactions are by or on behalf of a specific person and if they result in cash coming into or cash going out of the financial institution in an amount greater than $3,000 during any one business day. Where the $3,000 transaction floor is exceeded, the financial institution processing the transaction must complete a Money Order Transaction Report, Form 8105, reporting certain details about the transaction. Civil and criminal penalties are provided for failure to file the required report, or for filing a false or fraudulent report.

Any property involved in a violation of 18 USC 1956 (Laundering of Monetary Instruments) or 18 USC 1957 (Engaging in Monetary Transactions in Property Derived From Specified Unlawful Activity) can be seized if it is subject to forfeiture under federal law. Under Inspection Service forfeiture guidelines, the seized assets may be equitably shared with any federal, state, or local agency that participated directly in any of the acts which led to the seizure or forfeiture of the property.

Enormous influence and power is available to the criminals who launder money. It will take a concerted effort by many federal, state, and local law enforcement agencies to address the problem. U.S. Postal Inspectors are ready to share their resources with other agencies in this effort.

109

Mug Books

Mug books should be used when you do not have a definite suspect but the witness indicates an ability to recognize the perpetrator.

MAINTAINING THE MUG BOOKS

Each investigator unit is responsible for maintaining the mug books, although they should be available for use by all officers. The supervisor of each detective unit should select one of his officers to keep up the books on a regular basis. The officer in charge of the mug books should:

1. Include all photographs as received from the Identification Section
2. Make sure that each photo is properly "backed up" with the name, date of birth, height and weight, date photographed, and the photo identification number on the reverse side of the photograph
3. Cross out or cover with nontransparent tape any date appearing on the face of the photograph
4. Make sure that no information, other than the dates of birth, race, and sex of the photo subjects appear on the mug books in view of the witness; specifically, information about the crimes for which persons in the books were arrested should not be visible to the witness
5. Maintain a separate looseleaf binder containing the mug book record sheets. There should be a separate record sheet for each book. When a photo is placed in the mug book, the date of insertion, the photo identification number and name of the photo subject should be entered on the appropriate sheet. When a photo is permanently removed from the book, the date of its removal should be entered on the record sheet.

REMOVAL OF THE MUG BOOKS

Whenever it is necessary to remove mug books from the detectives' room, for example to show them to a witness in the hospital, you should notify the officer in charge of them so that other officers will be able to find out where they are and when they will be returned.

110

Offshore Private Banking

When investigating money laundering through offshore private banking it is necessary to understand who and what is involved. This includes private banking activities carried out by domestic and foreign banks operating in the United States that involve financial secrecy jurisdiction, such as establishing of accounts for offshore entities like private investment companies (PICs), offshore trusts, and private banking activities conducted by foreign branches of United States banks. Private investment companies are "shell" companies incorporated in financial secrecy jurisdictions that are formed to hold client assets. They are designed to keep their clients' confidentiality for various tax- or trust-related reasons. While most PICs are generally used for legitimate reasons, they may also camouflage money laundering and other illegal acts.

The authorities' reliance on financial institutions as the first line of defense against money laundering is based primarily upon the U.S. Treasury's Financial Crimes Enforcement Group and the enhanced suspicious activity reporting rules (since April 1, 1996), which are aimed at identifying transactions at or above $5,000 involving funds derived from illegal activities, transactions intended to disguise the nature of these funds by evading the Bank Secrecy Act requirements, and transactions that are not normal for the specific customer or client and appear to have no lawful business purpose. The banking authorities are expected through this effort to have a "know your customer" policy (KYC). Regulations are being developed to formalize such a policy.

The nine offshore jurisdictions are the Bahamas, Bahrain, Cayman Islands, Channel Islands, Hong Kong, Luxembourg, Panama, Singapore, and Switzerland. Of these, the Bahamas, Cayman Islands, Luxembourg, Panama, and Switzerland have bank secrecy laws that include criminal sanctions. Of the nine, Bahrain and Singapore do not allow United States judicial authorities access to individual customer information. All except Hong Kong and, with limited scope, Singapore, will not permit United States banking regulators to access individual customer information or to conduct on-site examinations. Bahrain stands out as the only offshore location that has no KYC policies or guidelines or requirement to report suspicious transactions.

Most of these banks are reluctant to share data due to the burdens placed upon them to know who and what. Of course, most of them also fear the loss of clients due to compromising their confidentiality. For a complete analysis of these concerns refer to the report *Money Laundering: Regulatory Oversight of Offshore Private Banking Activities*, Washington, D.C.: United States General Accounting Office, June, 1998.

111

Organized Crime

This can be one of the most misunderstood topics by the general population and by some private and public enforcement people. We believe that agreement on a clear and simple definition can aid the process of understanding and awareness. The definition of *organized crime* is: A criminal conspiracy engaged in commercial type crimes and schemes. These are both domestic and global in character. There is no distinction between race, creed, color, or national origin.

The basic goals of organized crime cartels include:

- Domination and control of major rackets and schemes
- Penetration, infiltration, and control of legitimate business
- Subversion of social and economic welfare of a country
- Corruption, graft, and political influence

Organized crime factions for their own benefit, welfare, and success can and do maintain an organized structure. They will collaborate and cooperate with other factions for mutual gain or support. These alliances are not limited by geographic location or any other differences. Their mutual concerns are to foster control and satisfy greed. The nomenclature may be very different on how the leadership is named, but each has its board of directors, stockholders, and methods of division of profits. Meetings are conducted both domestically and internationally to accomplish these goals, and in addition to:

- Settle disputes
- Reconfigure territories
- Access political influence, takeovers, and control
- Decide on methods to influence public opinion
- Determine organizational punishment

One of the modern era influences on the "war" on organized crime, at least in the United States, was the passing of the Omnibus Crime Bill in October 1970. This bill established the parameters for the use of technical listening devices. This law, along with the Racketeer Influenced and Corrupt Organization (known as civil and criminal RICO), which can award up to treble damages plus legal reimbursement cost, have had a tremendous impact on organized crime.

The citizens of any country tend to tolerate or accept organized crime because of ignorance. They are not aware of the various forms it can take or how far-reaching it can become. They may also benefit in some manner through their nonaction. No one can accurately estimate the extent of organized crime or the finesse it employs. An example of this is the well-established belief that if you need to get something accomplished, transported, safely delivered, constructed, or anything else associated with implementing a business in the new Russia, you need the partnership of organized crime.

Almost thirty years ago, the U.S. Chamber of Commerce, in its report "Marshaling Citizen Power Against Crime," stated: "A formidable problem faced by the nation's criminal justice system is insufficient citizen involvement. Indeed, why not leave the crime problem to the professionals? The answer is that the professionals themselves are aware and admit that without citizen involvement, they do not have the man power or funds to shoulder the monumental burden of combating crime." If we do nothing, the problems of organized crime and corruption will escalate and our government businesses, economy, families will suffer the consequences.

112

Phantom Employee Fraud

Payroll checks may be issued to fictitious or ex-employees by internal financial staff. It may also occur that actual employees are overpaid and the recipient "kicks back" to the internal coconspirator a portion of the overpayment. To document this type of fraud, it is necessary to do the following:

- Examine the personnel files of the suspect employees paying particular attention to the special security numbers and the W-2 tax withholding forms.
- Compare the social security number with the employee history and geographic place of issue.
- Compare the employee lists with payroll checks.
- Compare the payroll amounts with the employee's normal salary of record.
- Examine travel and expense vouchers and related documentation looking for uplifted amounts.

When your preliminary investigative findings are completed, it is time to examine the actual checks themselves. Assemble all the suspect's checks and do the following:

- Determine if the check(s) was cashed or deposited.
- Identify the endorser or endorsers.

- Look for other identifying support on the check such as a driver's license number.
- Obtain account statements.
- Identify other methods of money transfers such as money orders, traveler's checks, cashier's checks, wire transfers, and withdrawal ships.
- Identify all movements of the check beginning with where the deposit was made. The depository bank will stamp its identification on the rear of the check. Also appearing on the check will be the Federal Reserve Bank that processed the check for collection as well as the bank from which the check was drawn.

Documenting how funds have been moved and transferred builds a record to identify all the parties involved. The bank's copies of such items as cashier's checks and wire transfers will be important to the prosecution of a white collar fraud. These records may be subpoenaed.

113

Photographic Arrays

A *photographic array* is a group of selected photos that you may show to a witness when you have a definite suspect who is not in custody or when the subject is in custody but it is impractical to stage a lineup.

COMPOSITION OF THE PHOTOGRAPHIC ARRAY

1. The array should consist of only one photograph of the suspect and at least eight other photographs. The array should contain no more than six to twelve photographs. If, however, the suspect was placed in a lineup, a witness who did not view the lineup may be shown a photograph of the lineup without other photos.
2. If you have more than one suspect for the crime under investigation, you should show each suspect's photo in a separate array.
3. Each photograph in the array should be similar in type and size.
4. Each person in the photographs should be similar in age, sex, race, and as many other visible characteristics as possible.

5. The persons depicted in the photographs should not be wearing distinctive clothing or headwear.

PROCEDURES FOR CONDUCTING PHOTOGRAPHIC ARRAYS

1. *Photo Placement:* You should randomly place the suspect's photo among the other photographs in the array. The photographs may be laid out in a regular pattern on a surface in front of the witness, inserted into the pockets of a photo display page and then handed to the witness to examine, or the photos may be handed to the witness in a deck provided that the suspect's photo is neither on top or bottom.
2. "Blank Array: If you have a number of photographs of persons with physical characteristics similar to those of the suspect, you should consider using a *blank array*. That is, in addition to the array in which the suspect's photo appears, you may show the witness an array which does not contain the suspect's photograph. This will counter the witness's assumption that the suspect's picture appears in the array and thereby discourage the witness from selecting the photo that most resembles the perpetrator even though the witness cannot positively identify him.
3. *Second Array:* If the witness fails to identify the suspect from an array and a second array is to be shown to him, it should contain one or two other photographs from the first array in addition to the suspect's, and several new photographs.
4. You may include in a photo array, the photographs of persons about whom you desire to obtain information, even though they not suspected of the crime under investigation.

114

Photographs, Videos, and Sketches

These are tools used in investigations to reconstruct the scene or results of a crime. Because it is generally accepted that the average person remembers 80 to 90 percent of what he or she does after 24 hours, note taking will be the basis of your report and your notes should be legible, accurate, understandable and, of course, complete. The latter simply means that the notes should contain all the facts. They are a compilation of addresses, phone numbers, descriptions, measurements, supportive data pertaining to sketches, photographs, and videos. All of your notes should have correct spellings and/or should be spell checked.

Items to be included:

- Record dates, times, where you are, and the names of everyone present at the scene or interview.
- Sketches differ from photographs as the photograph shows everything and the sketch shows important details. Sketches can give clearer understanding of the scene or conditions. They outline facts and support photographs. Each sketch should specify where evidence is found.
- Scale recommendations for sketches:
    1/2 inch = 1 foot for small rooms
    1/4 inch = 1 foot for large rooms
    1/2 inch = 1 foot for very large rooms such as a convention floor or for buildings
    1/2 inch = 10 feet for large buildings
    1/2 inch = 10 feet for property
    1/8 inch = 10 feet for large area with or without buildings such as a campus or office park
- Sketches should be made before anything is moved, altered or destroyed.
- When taking photographs, a log should be kept to detail the object or reason for the photo.
- Photograph from left to right.
- It is recommended that there be at least one witness to observe you video or photograph the scene.
- Video in color whenever possible.
- Never write or mark photographs or videos. Photographs should be identified with labels placed on the back of the photo. Videos are labeled on the tape case.

115

Phrases and Proper Names You Should Know

- Felony
- Misdemeanor
- Probable cause/beyond a reasonable doubt
- Authority to arrest
- Arraignment/probation/parole
- District attorney/state attorney/U.S. Attorney
- Miranda warning
- Searches and seizures—Fourth Amendment
- Intentional liability/strict liability/civil liability/vicarious liability/gross liability
- EEOC—Equal Employment Opportunity Commission
- CFR—Code of Federal Regulations
- Exclusionary rule
- Self-incrimination—Fifth Amendment
- Corpus delecti
- Murder/voluntary and involuntary manslaughter/negligent manslaughter/homicide
- Assault/assault and battery (A&B)/aggravated assault
- Aggravated battery/felonious assault and battery
- Extortion
- Federal agencies—FBI, Secret Service, Alcohol, Tobacco, and Firearms (ATF), U.S. Marshals
- Statute of limitations
- Entrapment
- Comparative negligence/gross negligence
- White collar crime
- Armed/unarmed robbery
- Internal theft
- Uttering
- Fraud
- Blackmail
- Domestic violence/workplace violence
- Courts—district, superior, and federal
- U.S. Supreme Court

- Suspicious person
- Common law/common law crimes
- Statutory crimes
- *Terry v. Ohio/Mapp v. Ohio*
- Types of searches
- Polygraph examinations
- OSHA regulations
- Privacy Act/invasion of privacy
- Freedom of Information Act
- Federal Communication Act
- Confidential informants
- Scope of authority
- Subpoena/summons
- Affidavits/depositions

116

Pleadings and Evidence

The guidelines for pleadings and evidence are slightly different for private enforcement as compared to public enforcement. The most essential difference is that the private sector is not required to advise suspects on their Miranda privileges (the right to remain silent, etc.). We describe in this section the key elements when developing evidence and the process of pleading. This section is by no means complete as there are variations, particularly where international interests are involved.

It is important to establish the basic process for criminal and civil cases. Simply stated, the criminal process begins with a complaint and/or an indictment. The defense would respond with a plea of guilty, not guilty or *nolo contendere* (no contest). In civil cases, generally the main pleadings consist of a petition filed by the plaintiff and the defendant's answer. The points of disagreement will determine the question(s) at issue. A petition for an injunction is a request for the court to issue an order directing someone to discontinue his/her performance of an illegal act, which can be something as simple and personal as creating a disturbance to engaging in business interruption tactics.

Some classifications of evidence are:

Testimony: Oral testimony given under oath or affirmation in court by a living witness Circumstantial and Direct: Direct testimony is the testimony of an eye witness to the principal fact. Circumstantial testimony is any other evidence from which an inference may be drawn as it pertains to the issue.

Facts and Circumstances: A fact is what the witness himself or herself has seen, heard, felt, tasted, and/or smelled. Circumstances are collections of fact.

Conclusions: These are statements made by a witness that he or she believes but has not actually seen or knows by their own knowledge.

Hearsay: A witness attempts to tell what he or she does not know through personal experience but has only heard someone else express it.

Admissions and Confessions: Admission is a statement or act that amounts to affirming to some material fact against the person making it. Confessions are admissions of guilt voluntarily made by persons accused of having committed a crime.

117

Postal Inspection: Investigative Authority

The oldest federal law enforcement agency in the United States was founded in 1737. The Postal Inspection is a highly professional organization with broad investigative authority and unique abilities. They conduct both audits and investigations. They spend about two-thirds of their time investigating postal crimes. They have both a uniform force and armed federal agents who make felony arrests, serve federal warrants, and work closely with U.S. Attorneys. They also assist and support local, county, and state public and private enforcement.

There are over 2,000 Postal Inspectors who can assist public and private enforcement by:

- Assisting in investigations and in locating suspects and witnesses by providing information from postal records

- Instituting a mail cover to assist in locating a fugitive or investigation of felonies
- Assisting in obtaining a federal search warrant for, and making a controlled delivery of, mail containing illegal narcotics
- Assisting in child pornography investigations where the mail has been used to send or receive pornographic pictures
- Providing forensic analysis of evidence when working a joint investigation with other enforcement agencies

Federal laws on selected postal crimes include:

- 18 USC 876—Mailing threats and extortion letters
- 18 USC 912—Impersonating a postal worker
- 18 USC 1001—False statements to the government
- 18 USC 1029—Fraud via access device
- 18 USC 1302—Mailing lottery tickets and related items
- 18 USC 1341—Mail fraud
- 18 USC 1342—Using fictitious name or address in mail fraud
- 18 USC 1343—Fraud by wire, radio, television
- 18 USC 1461—Mailing obscene or crime-inciting matter
- 18 USC 1463—Mailing indecent matter on wrappers or envelopes
- 18 USC 1705—Destruction/vandalism to mail containers and mail
- 18 USC 1707—Theft of Postal Service property
- 18 USC 1708—Theft of mail or possession of stolen mail
- 18 USC 1735—Mailing sexually oriented advertisements
- 18 USC 2114—Robbery of post office or employee
- 18 USC 2115—Burglary of a post office
- 18 USC 2252—Mailing child pornography
- 21 USC 812—Schedules of controlled substances
- 21 USC 843(b)—Unlawful mailing of a controlled substance
- 39 USC 3005—False representation statute
- 39 USC 3010—Mailing of unordered merchandise

118

Private and Public Sector Differences[76]

The fundamental difference between the investigative process in the public and in the private sectors is the *objective*. The primary objective of investigations in the public sector is to serve the interests of society. If those interests are best served by removing or otherwise punishing those who commit offenses against the public good, then the reconstructive method of investigation is used. When the purpose of the investigation is to inhibit and suppress criminal activity—prostitution and gambling are two examples—then constructive, covert techniques are employed.

The primary objective of the investigative process in the private sector is to serve the interests of the organization, not society as a whole. If those interests are best served by removing or otherwise punishing those who criminally attack the organization, or whose performance in any way defeats or impedes organizational goals, the reconstructive strategy is used where the conduct is a matter of history. Where that conduct or activity is ongoing, constructive, covert techniques must be applied.

It is interesting to note that what serves the best interests of society may not necessarily serve the best interests of the organization, and vice versa. For example, the society's interests are protected when an embezzler is prosecuted and sentenced to prison. There are occasions, however, when the embezzler, having banked all his thefts, would be happy to return the stolen funds in order to avoid prosecution. Such an agreement would be unacceptable in the public sector. A seasoned private sector investigator, on the other hand, is not primarily concerned with prosecution and sentencing. Recovery of the loss might be a more important achievement, better serving the interests of the private organization.

More often than not, investigations in the private sector that deal with criminal behavior result in serving the public sector's objective as well as the organization's despite the fact that there is a fundamental difference in the perception of the crime. Wherein lies that perceptual difference? It comes from differing views of the victim. The public investigator sees society as the victim, whereas the corporate investigator views his organization as the victim.

More specifically, forgery detectives in a metropolitan police force consider forgers to be a general menace to the community. Investigators of a banking institution or credit-granting company regard forgers, whose target is their organization, as very real, immediate threats to the financial stability of the organization.

From the viewpoint of the private investigator, the forger must be stopped not because he is breaking the law, but because he is damaging or victimizing the organization.

Different perceptions and different objectives have a direct impact on the strategies and the character of the investigative process in the two sectors, leading to other differences. Public investigators are usually armed, for example, while private investigators are unarmed. Other interesting differences that invite comparison require more examination.

SOURCE OF AUTHORITY AND FUNDING

The public investigator represents the sovereignty of government, whose authority is vested in constitutional and statutory law. Its efforts are financed by public funds, replenished through taxation.

The private investigator represents management, with some authority derived from statutory and case laws. The same authority is afforded to any citizen, such as the power to make arrests under certain conditions, although that power and authority are unknown to most private citizens. In addition, the private security investigator has delegated authority from senior company management.

SOURCES OF INFORMATION

In the public view, there are relatively few limitations to such information as criminal records, government records and files at municipal, county, state and federal levels. On the other hand, there are accelerating limitations to private access to public records.

119

The Public Defender System[77]

Public defender programs may be administered either statewide or locally. Under a statewide system, a chief defender is appointed by the governor or the judiciary. He or she is charged with providing the system of representation for each of the counties in the state. The chief defender usually establishes branch offices staffed by his or her assistants, although contractual arrangements with local law firms may be used by some counties. The local branches are subject to supervisory authority of the chief defender and receive support services from the central office. Local defender agencies are organized by the county or judicial district. Most are government agencies, but some are private nonprofit organizations receiving funding from the local courts or the community. (Y. Kamisar, W. R. LaFave, and G. Israel. *Basic Criminal Procedure.* St. Paul, MN: West Publishing Co., 1986).

The public defender is more often than not a full-time county, state, or federal government employee. He or she earns a fixed salary and specializes in criminal law representing criminal indigents. The public defender position is particularly popular in urban areas, and it has become increasingly popular in smaller jurisdictions. Twenty-three states have adopted the public defender system. The size of the public defender office is directly proportional to the constituency that the system serves. In a rural setting there may be but one public defender, whereas in a major metropolitan setting, there are usually hundreds.

120

Qualities of the Investigator[78]

To the uninitiated, the aspirant, and the distant observer, there is an aura of romanticism surrounding the investigator and his work. That illusion is quickly dispelled in the light of reality. The real world of investigative work is hard, demanding, and rarely glamorous. Occasionally, a case may come along that is exciting, or in which the answers come easily, but as a rule investigation is a tedious, exhausting, frustrating, time-consuming, and sometimes dirty (in the literal sense) process. Invariably, the novice investigator is somewhat dismayed by the difference between his or her preconceptions of the nature of the work and the reality.

Crimes are not solved by ingenious and clever supersleuths but by hardworking men and women who share one common denominator: perseverance. In the words of Samuel Johnson, "Great works are performed, not by strength, but perseverance." This investigative virtue is defined as "holding to a course of action, belief, or purpose without giving way; steadfastness ... continuing strength or patience in dealing with something arduous. It particularly implies withstanding difficulty or resistance" in striving for a goal.[79]

Perseverance is the one overriding human trait or characteristic among the many deemed necessary, or at least highly desirable, for investigative work. What are the others? One authority, Donald Schultz, lists 15 "desirable attributes of an investigator." Charles O'Hare boils it down to three: character, judgment, and the ability to deal with people. The familiar "green book," *Municipal Police Administration*, has its own list, including "the ability to be deceptive." Collating, modifying, deleting, and adding to the suggestions in these sources, we have identified 21 qualities or characteristics that are necessary in the effective investigator. Invariably, a successful investigator, man or woman, will possess, in varying degrees, each of these traits, either as innate or learned qualities. He or she is:

1. Observant
2. Resourceful
3. Patient
4. People-oriented
5. Understanding of human behavior
6. Knowledgeable about legal implications of the work
7. A skilled communicator
8. Receptive
9. Possessed of a sense of well-being
10. Dedicated to the work
11. A self-starter
12. Skeptical
13. Intuitive
14. Energetic
15. A good actor
16. Capable of sound judgment
17. Logical
18. Intelligent
19. Creatively imaginative
20. Of good character
21. Professional

121

Racketeer Influenced and Corrupt Organizations: Civil RICO

The Federal RICO Statute (Title 18, U.S. Code, Section 1961) and state "little RICO" laws are often used in fraud and corruption cases. The basic elements of a typical RICO fraud case (18 USC 1962)) are:

- The defendant was a "person"
- Associated with an "enterprise"
- Engaged in or affecting interstate commerce
- Who conducted the affairs of the enterprise through a "pattern of racketeering activity"; that is, two or more predicate violations (listed in Section 1961), which include, among others, mail and wire fraud, interstate transportation of property taken by fraud (18 USC 2314), and bribery related offenses

The key elements—the "enterprise" and "pattern of racketeering activity"— are the subject of much case law which varies by jurisdiction. Ideally, the "enterprise" should be an entity with an identity and purpose separate and distinct from the defendants and the criminal acts charged in the indictment, and the "pattern of racketeering activity" should include a series of distinct criminal episodes or schemes, rather than, for example, two mailings in what is essentially a single fraud.

The federal and many state RICO statutes also provide for forfeiture of ill-gotten gains and civil remedies, including injunctions, dissolution of the criminal enterprise, treble damages, and the award of attorney fees to the prevailing plaintiff.

A civil action for damages or injunctive relief under the RICO statute or otherwise may be brought by the government or private parties in virtually any fraud or corruption case. A civil complaint provides a number of advantages which make it an attractive alternative to criminal prosecution in many white collar cases:

- In some white collar cases incarceration is unlikely or for a minimal term. Money damages (including RICO treble damages or punitive damages) may be an adequate remedy. And, if the defendant violates an injunction or other court order, a jail term for contempt may be imposed.

- Civil cases require a much lower burden of proof: mere preponderance of the evidence (which may be ever so slight), or a clear and convincing standard, rather than the much more stringent criminal burden.
- The Fifth Amendment privilege against self-incrimination does not apply in civil cases. A defendant may still refuse to answer questions or produce personal documents, but his failure to do so may be considered as evidence against him, or result in sanctions, including the entry of a judgment against him.
- Civil actions provide broad discovery rights, which may lay the foundation for later criminal charges. (A civil action may not be brought as a ruse merely to obtain evidence for a criminal case, however.)
- Civil cases permit the joinder of claims and defendants, such as multiple episodes of fraudulent conduct, which would be considered prejudicial in a criminal case.
- RICO civil actions permit the recovery of court costs and attorney fees by the prevailing plaintiff.
- A defendant convicted of a criminal RICO violation is "estopped" (precluded) from denying the essential elements of the criminal offense in a subsequent RICO civil suit. This usually means the only issue in the civil case is the amount of damages.

122

The Real Problems in American Justice[80]

1. Dangerous suspects commit crimes while awaiting trials on other charges. Defendants have a legal right to be considered for release before trial, and nearly two-thirds of those charged with serious crimes—including one-fourth of accused murderers—are allowed out on the street while awaiting trial. While most of them stay out of trouble, a disturbingly high one out of three either is rearrested, fails to appear in court on time, or commits some infraction that results in bail revocation.

2.   Prosecutors make bargains with too many criminals. In nine cases out of ten, no trial is ever held. The defendants' accept plea bargains that let them plead guilty, usually to just a few of the charges. Critics argue that to move cases along, prosecutors too readily abandon charges that could bring tougher penalties. Although that does happen, just as common is overcharging—filing counts of dubious provability to pressure defendants.

3.   Criminal cases take too long. The interval between arrest and sentencing averages 274 days nationwide for murders and 172 days for violent crimes generally. The length of the few cases that go to trial is less of a problem. The National Center for State Courts reports that trials average about 11 hours, much shorter than the time it took for single witnesses to testify in the Simpson extravaganza. Murder trials typically last one to two weeks, depending on the circumstances. California trials tend to take longer.

Still, "we can do a lot better" at expediting cases once they reach court, says Barry Mahoney of the Denver-based Justice Management Institute. Mahoney's group and others offer trial-management training to judges, but probably fewer than 10 percent nationwide have taken it. A bigger problem: there aren't enough judges to juggle all witnesses, defendants, and lawyers that come to court.

123

The Rules of Evidence[81]

Rules of evidence govern the presentation of evidence at a trial in much the same way that the rules of a game govern the conduct of the players and, continuing with this analogy, the judge acts as impartial referee or umpire. Evidence consists of legal proofs presented to the court in the form of witnesses, records, documents, objects, and other means, for the purpose of influencing the opinions of the judge or jury toward the case of the prosecution or the defense. The four kinds of evidence are:

1.   Real evidence: Real evidence refers to objects of any kind (weapons, clothing, fingerprints, and so on). Real evidence must be the original evidence, the original objects. Reasonable facsimiles such as photographs, reproductions,

or duplicates that are necessitated by practical considerations may also be introduced as real evidence.

2. Testimonial evidence: Testimonial evidence is the statements of competent, sworn witnesses. All real evidence must be accompanied by testimonial evidence.

3. Direct evidence: Direct evidence refers to the observations of eyewitnesses.

4. Circumstantial evidence: Circumstantial evidence comprises any information that tends to prove or disprove a point at issue. Circumstantial evidence proves a subsidiary fact from which the existence of the ultimate fact in the criminal trial—the guilt or innocence of the accused—may be inferred.

To be accepted by the court, evidence must be relevant, competent, and material. Relevant evidence directly pertains to the issues in question. That is, evidence is relevant not only when it tends to prove or disprove a fact at issue, but also when it establishes facts from which further inferences can be drawn.

Whether the defendant "did it" is not relevant to his or her successful prosecution. What is relevant—the only thing that is relevant—is the prosecution's ability to produce admissible evidence to prove the defendant's guilt beyond a reasonable doubt. Sometimes this is problematic, especially when dealing with the human factor.

124

Screening and Case Assignment[82]

Every morning, incident reports are assembled from the previous day and distributed to the appropriate investigative unit. The assignment of an investigator to a case is determined by the organizational pattern of the department; for example, assignments might be made by crime specialty (e.g., homicide, robbery, burglary, sex offenses) or by geographic area. Specialization might be so detailed that assignment personnel can direct an incident report to the specific investigator who will handle that case. Otherwise, the report goes to a unit supervisor who assigns the case to a detective in his or her unit, based on previous assignments or individual work loads. Each detective usually receives one or two new cases a day. Work loads are lower for detectives who handle crimes against the person, higher for those who handle minor property crimes.

In some departments, formal "solvability factors" and the judgment of the unit supervisor are used to determine if a specific case should be followed up by an investigator or suspended until new facts develop. Generally, however, every case is assigned to a responsible investigator, with some minimal attempt at follow up expected. This minimal effort is usually an attempt to contact the victim to obtain facts in addition to those recorded in the incident report. Although most investigators have 20 or 30 open cases on their desks at any one time, only two or three cases are really considered active. Work load data show that most cases are closed within the first day of activity, and very few remain active after two or three days.

125

The Security Function[83]

SECURITY, PUBLIC POLICE, AND THE CONSTITUTION

The framers of the U.S. Constitution, with their grievances against England uppermost in mind when creating a new government, were primarily concerned with the manner in which the powerless citizen was, or could be, abused by the enormous power of government. The document they drew up was concerned, therefore, not with the rights of citizens as against each other, but with those rights with respect to federal or state action. Breaking and entering by one citizen upon another may be criminal and subject to tort action as well, but it is not a violation of any constitutional right. Similar action by public police is a clear violation of Fourth Amendment rights and, as such, is expressly forbidden by the Constitution.

The public police have substantially greater powers than security personnel in their powers of arrest, detention, search, and interrogation. Where security people are, as a rule, limited to the premises of their employer, public police operate through a much wider jurisdiction. At the same time, the public police are limited by various restrictions imposed by the Constitution. Although the issue is not entirely clear, private police are not, as a rule, touched by these same restrictions.

Public police are limited by federal statutes, which make it a crime for officials to deny others their constitutional rights. The Fourth and Fourteenth Amendments are most frequently invoked as the cornerstones in citizen protection against arbitrary police action.

The Fourth Amendment guarantees that "the right of the people to be secure in their persons, houses, papers, and effects, against unreasonable searches and seizures, shall not be violated, and no Warrants shall issue, but upon probable cause, supported by Oath or affirmation, and particularly describing the place to be searched, and the persons or things to be seized."

SECURITY'S PLACE IN THE ORGANIZATION

The degree and nature of the authority vested in the security manager become matters of the greatest importance when such a function is fully integrated into the organization. Any evaluation of the scope and authority required by security to perform effectively must consider a variety of factors, both formal and informal, that exist in the structure.

Definition of Authority

It is management's responsibility to establish the level of authority at which security may operate in order to accomplish its mission. It must have authority to deal with the establishment of security systems. It must be able to conduct inspections of performance in many areas of the company. It must be in a position to evaluate performance and risk throughout the company.

All such authority relationships, of course, should be clearly established by management and made with the assistance and guidance of a professional consultant. This trend has caused a growth in the number of security consultants, particularly independent consultants who do not have a vested interest in the outcome of their recommendations.

Determining costs and effectiveness is only the first step. Having done this, management will then have to face the important question of whether security can be truly and totally integrated into the organization. If, upon analysis, it is found that the existing structure would, in some way, suffer from the addition of new organizational functions, alternatives to the integrated proprietary security department must be sought. These alternatives usually consist only of the application and supervision of physical security measures. This inevitably results in the fragmentation of protective systems in the various areas requiring security. However, these alternatives are sometimes effective, especially in those firms whose overall risk and vulnerability are low. But as the crime rates continues to climb, and as criminal methods of attack and the underground network of distribution continue to become more sophisticated, anything less than total integration will become increasingly more inadequate.

Once management has recognized that existing problems—real or potential—make the introduction or enlargement of security a necessity for continued effective operation, it is obliged to exert every effort to create an atmosphere in which security can exert its full efforts to accomplish stated company objectives. Any equivocation by management at this point can only serve to weaken or to ultimately undermine the security effectiveness that might be obtained by a clearer statement of total support and directives resulting in intracompany co-operation with security efforts.

Levels of Authority

Obviously, there are many mixtures of authority levels at which the security managers operate. Their functional authority may encompass a relatively limited area, prescribed by broad outlines of basic company policy. In matters of investigation, they may be limited to a staff function in which they may advise and recommend or even assist in conducting the investigation, but they would not have direct control or command over the routines of employees.

It is customary for security managers to exercise line authority over preventive activities of the company. In this situation, they command the guards, who in turn command the employees in all matters over which security managers have jurisdiction. Security managers will, of course, have full line authority over the conduct of their own departments, within which they too, will have staff personnel as well as those to whom they have delegated functional authority.

The Power of Security Personnel

Security personnel are generally limited to the exercise of powers possessed by every citizen. There is no legal area where the position of a security officer, as such, confers any greater rights, powers, or privileges than those possessed by every other citizen. A few states, for example Michigan, confer additional arrest powers for security personnel after the completion of 135 hours of training. As a practical matter, if the officer is uniformed he or she will very likely find that in most cases people will comply with his or her requests. Many people are not aware of their own rights nor of the limitations of powers of a security officer. Thus, a security officer can obtain compliance to directives that may be, if not illegal, beyond his or her power to command. This acquiescence is usually harmless, but in cases where a security officer has unwisely taken liberties with his or her authority, the officer and the officer's employer will be subject to the penalties of a tort action. The litigation involved in suing a security officer and his or her employer for tortious conduct is slow and expensive, which may make such recourse impossible for the poor and those unfamiliar with their rights. But the judgments that have been awarded have had a generally sobering effect on security professionals, and have probably served to reduce the number of such incidents.

Criminal law also regulates security activities. Major crimes such as battery, manslaughter, kidnapping, and breaking and entering—any one of which may be confronted in the course of security activities—are substantially deterred by criminal sanctions.

Further limitations may be imposed upon the authority of a security force by licensing laws, administrative regulations, and specific statutes directed at security activities. Operating contracts between employers and security firms may also specify limits on the activities of the contracted personnel.

126

Seizures, Plain View[84]

Police can seize contraband from a vehicle if three clearly defined criteria are met. First, officers must be prepared to prove that they were lawfully in the place where the observations were made. Second, they must observe something that they know to be subject to seizure. In most cases this will be contraband, such as an illegal firearm or some type of drug. Finally, the item must be readily observable. The requirement that the item be in the open is the reason why this act is referred to as a seizure and not a search. If the officer had to look for the item, then it is a search and cannot be justified as a plain view seizure (*Coolidge v. New Hampshire*, 403 U.S. 443 (1974); *Brown v. Texas*, 443 U.S. 47 (1979)).

In *Colorado v. Bannister*, an officer approached a car parked in a gas station that he had earlier seen being driven at excessive speed. As he approached, two men got out of the car. The officer asked the driver for his license and looked through the window on the driver's side. The interior of the car was illuminated by lights from the station. The officer saw chrome lug nuts on the console between the bucket seats and two lug wrenches on the floorboard. Similar items had been reported stolen earlier in the area. The officer then realized that the men matched the description of suspects in the reported theft of auto parts. The suspects were arrested and the items seized. The Court held that the evidence was in plain view and the seizure was valid (*Colorado v. Bannister*, 449 U.S. 1 (1980)).

127

Sentencing, Appeals and the Death Penalty[85]

Sentencing is perhaps the most important phase of the criminal justice process for the criminal defendant as well as for the public at large. It is at this stage that the disposition of the criminal offender is decided. In earlier periods of American history, offenders were subject to retaliation by physical abuse as punishment for wrongdoing. Contemporary criminal justice is still punitive in its orientation, but its procedures are justified on several theoretical grounds, including retribution, deterrence, and incapacitation.

Until recent years, the goals of rehabilitation and reintegration also were part of the punitive decision. However, with the advent of the new conservatism and the brutal reality of "warehousing" as the predominant correctional procedure in the eighties and nineties, tremendous popular support has grown for the position that retribution ("the law of just deserts") is the most important objective of sentencing.

Traditional sentences include fines, probation, and imprisonment. Probation is the most common choice. The sentencing structure itself has been riddled with disparity and problems. Also, due to massive prison overcrowding, citizens have become frustrated with the criminal courts convicting defendants and sentencing them to long terms in prison, only to find the criminals have served but a fraction of the sentence that was imposed on them. In response, legislators have introduced sentencing guidelines and formulated sentencing councils and commissions to rethink the whole sentencing process. One of the most significant features of sentencing is its tripod structure, involving the legislature, a judge, and a correctional agency. The actions of each of these parties affect the type and length of sentence imposed on the offender. The system often results in sentence disparity in which the courts seek to fit the sentence to the individual offender rather than to the crime.

Regardless of the accused's sentence, certain appeals are granted to him or her based on his or her sentence, as well as postconviction remedies. Historically, only on rare occasions have sentences imposed by courts been overturned for being excessive. Recently, however, under the sentencing guidelines, if trial judges choose to go outside the guidelines when sentencing defendants, their sentences are subject to automatic review by appellate courts and are often reversed.

The most serious sentence imposed by American criminal courts is the death penalty. Once thought to be no longer part of American law, the death penalty is gaining strength at an astonishing rate. Over 80 percent of Americans support the use of a death penalty. Yet for the state to take a life, such action must be theoretically justified. The justification for capital punishment has been hotly debated. Proponents argue capital punishment acts as a deterrent for the individual as well as for other potential murderers. Furthermore, capital punishment, they say, is the only satisfactory retribution that society can gain for such a heinous act as premeditated murder. Opponents argue that sentences are imposed arbitrarily, often based on the race of the victim. They also point out that there are many instances in American history where the death penalty has mistakenly been imposed. Such a mistake, these opponents argue, justifies the elimination of the death penalty altogether. Finally, they point out that all of the empirical studies on the subject have failed to prove that the death penalty acts as a deterrent. Other minor issues in the capital punishment debate have come forward but for the most part do not deserve much scholarly attention.

128

Shoplifting Surveillance[86]

As shoplifting is a covert crime, the action of the sneak thief, so is its detection a covert strategy. It is a very difficult strategy to learn and practice. Good shoplifting investigators, more commonly referred to as either detectives or operatives, are hard to find. Many candidates are trained but few develop into outstanding achievers. Those who do are aware of their skills and are frequently difficult to supervise. They are typically people of exceptional courage, having been in many scrapes while making arrests. Most have seen more criminal acts performed than a police officer with the same years of work experience. They love their work, and will turn down promotional opportunities if the promotion will take them "off the floor." They are deserving of great respect and admiration.

In shoplifting surveillance, knowledge of techniques used by the shoplifter is as important as the detective's own stratagems. Following is a list of some shoplifting strategies.

1. Put merchandise on and wear it out as though it belongs to the wearer. In some cases, women will come into a store wearing only underwear under a

buttoned up coat. They will then put on a dress, belt, and sweater after removing the price tags and wear the merchandise out of the store.

2. Put merchandise on beneath one's outer garments and wear the stolen items out concealed. A lot of swimwear and intimate apparel is stolen this way.

3. Place soft, folded items such as sweaters under the coat and armpit.

4. Push items off a counter so they fall into a waiting shopping bag.

5. Place articles in the bag of a previous purchase.

6. Carry into the store empty bags of the same or other stores and fill these bags with items while the shoplifter is shielded behind piles or racks of merchandise or in the privacy of a fitting room.

7. Hand merchandise to children who accompany you and let the children carry it out.

8. Wear special "boosting" coats that have hooks sewn on the inside to accommodate soft goods that are quickly placed there.

9. Wear special "boosting" coats that have a modified lining that makes the whole coat a huge pocket.

10. Carry "booster" boxes into the store. Such boxes appear to be ready to mail, wrapped and string-tied, or they may be disguised as fancy gift boxes. They are empty and have a false or trapdoor, or the bottom or side may be fitted with a spring-type hinge. Push the goods in and the false side gives way; withdraw the hand and the side snaps back to its original position.

11. Wear special "booster" bloomers, similar to old-fashioned ladies' underwear that comes down just above the knee. The legs of the garment are tied, or strong elastic is used so that stolen merchandise will not slip out. Stolen goods are pushed down the front of the bloomers, or an accomplice can push goods down the back.

12. Hide stolen items in the crotch area. Even items as bulky as a fur coat or several men's suits folded up can be hidden in this way between the thighs of a woman wearing a long, full skirt or dress, who then simply walks out of the store after concealing the items. Even typewriters have been removed in this fashion.

13. Switch price tags. A garment's $50.00 price tag is replaced by a $25.00 tag from another item, and the more expensive article is then purchased at the lower price. Similar switching is often done with boxed items. For example, four cubes of margarine are removed from the package and replaced with four cubes of pure butter, which is then purchased at the price of the margarine.

14. Pick up merchandise and immediately take it to a clerk, demanding your money back.

15. Run into the store, grab items and run out to a waiting car, catching everyone by surprise (if you are noticed at all).

129

Sketching Crime Scenes[87]

As with crime scene photographs, the purpose of crime scene sketches is to aid the jury in their attempt to understand how a crime occurred. Photographs are a valuable aid to the prosecution, but they are two-dimensional and may not show a relationship between objects. In addition, key items of evidence may not be sufficiently distinct in a photo, and thus it may lose some of its impact on the jury. Crime scene sketches are the simplest yet most effective means to illustrate the relationship of significant items of evidence to each other.

Crime scene sketches are of two types—rough and finished. Rough sketches are made by investigators at the scene. They need not be drawn to scale but must include accurate measurements. Graph paper is useful when drawing rough sketches. A finished sketch should be drawn to scale and should include the following information:

- Title of the sketch
- Date and time the crime occurred
- North represented by an arrow
- Outline of the crime scene
- Doors, windows, and other relevant items
- Legend
- Scale
- Identification of the officer who prepared the sketch

130

Sketching Preparation[88]

When preparing a diagram of the scene, it is important to remember that the purpose of the sketch is to aid the trier of fact to understand how the crime occurred. An effort should be made to eliminate extraneous items. The person preparing the sketch should determine what is essential to aid the jury's understanding.

131

Sketching, Measurements For[89]

All measurements should be made from permanent fixed objects, such as buildings, telephone poles, or trees. Indoor measurements should be made from specific points, such as corners or doors. When measuring an object so that it can later be returned to its original position, it is necessary to take measurements from two positions to two points on the item. For example, when measuring the location of a gun, measurements should be made from the butt *and* from the muzzle of the weapon. All measurements should be double-checked and verified before completing the sketch and submitting it as evidence. Objects on the sketch should be marked and recorded on the legend.

132

Sketches, Types of Crime Scene[90]

FLOOR PLAN

The floor plan sketch is basically a drawing of the major items found at the scene. It may be useful to prepare one sketch of the outline of the scene and then to make a number of photocopies of the original. The investigator sketching the scene can then add items to the photocopies as needed. It may also be helpful to make sketches on clear acetate overlays, on which additional relevant items are added.

EXPLODED OR CROSS-PROJECTION

The cross-projection sketch is an extension of the floor plan sketching technique, with the walls of the crime scene included in the diagram. The cross-projection sketch is drawn from an angle that resembles looking down at a shoe box, in which the walls of the crime scene are analogous to the sides of the shoe box. The sides of the box may then be cut and laid flat so that the jury can see the relationship of objects to each other. This type of sketch is particularly useful for showing important evidence such as blood stains and bullet holes.

MIDLINE

Crime scene sketches often become cluttered with too many lines and items. One way to avoid this is to use a midline sketching system, in which the investigator preparing the sketch divides the area to be sketched into two or four equal parts, similar to a zone search. A steel tape is then stretched through the room or subdivided parts of the room. The investigator can then measure the position of particular items of evidence from appropriate points on the tape measure.

133

Skills of the Successful Interviewer

What does the individual investigator need to have in order to be an effective and successful interviewer? When suspects and witnesses are managed efficiently and treated appropriately, the results produce more complete information. The outcome is accomplished faster and generally at less cost, inconvenience, disruption, and far less effort. In order to accomplish this you need to possess the ability to adopt a variety of personality traits, adjusting your character to blend with or dominate the varied traits and moods of the subjects in your interviews. Obviously, it is helpful if you have developed some acting skills and abilities. Your efforts should be determined by the emotions and attitudes you are confronted with by the object of your interview. If your subject shows remorse, then you become sympathetic without becoming emotional yourself. If hostility and anger are demonstrated, your attitude becomes stern. In all cases you must maintain an open mind and become a sponge for all information that is forthcoming. Never be judgmental and form conclusions about your suspect or witness—it will shut down the flow of information. Remember to be a better actor to overcome and control your personal feelings. You must always control your own prejudices.

Absolutely never attempt to impress your suspect, witness, or knowledgeable source. If questions are asked in a manner which is designed to impress the subject, you are in danger of getting less information than you should. The subject of the interview is making judgments of you and can easily take control. Suppress your own emotions and apply all your faculties in order to obtain your objective.

Never underestimate the mental or physical abilities of the object of your interview or interrogation. You must accept that at different points during the interview the capacities of your suspect may exceed your own. Always operate under the belief that the person being interviewed or interrogated is intelligent. Avoid showing any degree of contempt unless it is used as a ploy to gain specific information or as a tactic.

Items to avoid:

- Ridicule
- Bully or harassment
- Sneering or leering
- Abuse

- Making promises you can't keep
- Using offensive language
- Belittling the subject or their information
- Self-important
- Failing to listen
- Shouting, yelling, screaming, or raising your voice
- Joking, wise cracking, or making light of the situation—it can be misinterpreted

134

Sources of Investigative Information

Identifying sources of information can be limited only by your own lack of imagination. The following list is a partial compilation of documentary sources. Elsewhere in this book, you will find Internet addresses for online research and investigative sources.

- Alphabetic/geographic telephone directories
- Bank accounts/records of transactions
- Bankruptcies, liens, and judgments
- Credit data
- Financial history
- Public utilities subscriber lists
- Insurance companies
- Death record search
- Magazines, newspapers, biographical listings such as professional affiliations
- Criminal records search
- Corporation records
- Education verification
- Fraternal, labor, veterans, social, and political organizations
- Health clubs and other recreational types of clubs and facilities including public and private golf courses
- Car dealers, repair and gas stations

- Laundry marks and dry cleaning tags
- Hotels, restaurants, bars, lounges, and fast food chains and take out services
- Real estate agents and building associations
- Transportation modes—taxis, airlines, any other means possible where passenger lists and trip reports are maintained
- Bonding and security companies
- Various licensing bureaus of local, state, and federal governments
- Data banks
- Physicians and particular prescriptions or medications needed
- Post office
- Passport records
- Import/export license, U.S. Customs and Commerce
- Immigration and Naturalization Service
- U.S. Customs maintains records of all importers and exporters, custom house brokers and custom house trackmen
- Veterans' Administration
- Real property asset searches
- City, county and state records and vital statistics pertaining to land transfers, automobile and driver's information, births, deaths, marriages, board of elections records, occupancy and business privileges licenses, criminal records, civil and criminal litigation, real property tax assessments, and any liens or chattel mortgages

These are some of the numerous sources of investigative data that are available through legitimate means to you as an investigator. When seeking information and data it is recommended that you explain the need and use to be made of the information. Assure the holder that the data will be kept in confidence. If it is necessary to produce records for use in court, the holder should be issued a subpoena.

135

Specialized Security Equipment[91]

Specialized equipment is available to enhance the efficiency of the security force. The director of security should obtain or seek funding for any equipment required to improve the security program. Items in this category include cameras, binoculars, portable lights, night-vision devices, surveillance cameras, listening devices, flashlights, portable radios, first-aid kits, traffic-control devices, and special clothing for the health, comfort, or safety of security personnel. The office of security must keep abreast of new equipment that may improve the effectiveness of the security program. All items of security equipment for the use of security personnel or other individuals (appropriate clothing, self-protection devices, radios, handcuffs, and so on) will be procured by the office of security and issued to approved members of the security force.

136

Stakeouts[92]

Stakeouts usually occur when police have a tip that a crime is likely to occur at a specific location or when crime analysis pattern identification information leads them to believe that a crime may occur at one or more potential targets. In the case of a tip, it is advisable to substitute an undercover police officer in place of a potential victim, such as a clerk or salesperson. Trained police officers are better prepared to deal with dangerous situations. In addition, police have both an ethical and legal obligation to protect innocent persons in situations where they might be harmed. In *United States v. Watson* the Supreme Court held that police do not need an arrest warrant to apprehend a suspect who commits a crime in a public place. Thus, if police actually observe a robbery of a liquor store, for example, they may take the suspect into custody as soon as it is safely possible to do.

When a suspect is identified after the robbery has taken place, police need to make the arrest as soon as possible. As soon as the suspect is known, police obtain an arrest warrant for that individual. Legally, the officer's actions are guided by two cases, *Payton v. New York* and *Steagald v. United States*. In *Payton* the Court held that police must, in the absence of exigent or emergency circumstances, obtain an arrest warrant for a suspect before they may enter a private residence to make a felony arrest. In *Steagald* the Court ruled that an arrest warrant does not authorize police to enter a third party's home to make a felony arrest. Thus, if police believe that a suspect can be found in a residence other than that of the suspect, they must obtain a search warrant to enter the other residence to arrest the felon.

137

Substantive Criminal Law[93]

To understand the problem of crime, one must examine the broader issue of deviance from societal norms. Society's attempt to contain crime through controls (sanctions) range from informal disapproval to the use of the police powers of the state. Studies of antisocial attitudes, eccentricities, and various kinds of atypical behavior may all have potential value in helping to illuminate the factors involved in criminal conduct. All criminal acts are deviant, but not all deviant acts are criminal. Thus, only those deviant acts that legislative bodies have defined by statute as criminal may be legitimately considered crimes.

American criminal law as analyzed in this section combines the features of two systems: the common law, which developed in England, was transported to America and is based on the interpretation of judicial decisions; and statutory law, which is based on specific codes that are written and enacted by legislative bodies. These two sources are continually being transformed by American case law, which analyzes the meaning and significance of legislative statutes in the common law tradition. These systems are the basis of substantive criminal law, which define necessary elements of crimes and specify the penalties for their commission.

Offenses are generally classified as felony or misdemeanor crimes, depending on how they are punished. Felonies are punishable by death or imprisonment for one or more years. Misdemeanors are punishable by fines and less than one year in jail. There are also several subclassifications of the various substantive crimes. Several crimes constitute the law of homicide; at least five crimes fit into the category of crimes against the person; arson and burglary are the crimes against habitation; as many as six separate crimes constitute the acquisition offenses; and there are at least five crimes grouped under the general category of crimes against morality. American prosecutors are devoting extraordinary resources and energy to prosecuting acts that were not even considered criminal until the 1960s. Fighting environmental crime, for example, requires the coordination of many governmental and private agencies to achieve success.

We have studied each crime by defining the various elements that together constitute a particular criminal offense. The significance of analyzing each crime as to its constitutive elements relates to the issue of proof. The burden of proof is on the government to prove the defendant guilty beyond a reasonable doubt; what this means in effect is that the government has the burden of proving beyond a reasonable doubt every element that makes up the crimes with which the defendant is charged. This means that if a defendant is charged with a crime like burglary, which has seven elements, and if the government proves six of these elements beyond a reasonable doubt but the jury has a reasonable doubt as to the seventh element, the jury must find the defendant not guilty.

138

Surveillance

Surveillance is the secretive and continuous watching of persons, vehicles, places, or objects to obtain information concerning the activities and identities of an individual(s) or condition(s). There are two types of surveillance:

1. Moving: Follow the subject on foot or in a conveyance
2. Stationary: Continuous watching of a place, object, or person from a fixed point

It is important to accept that the criminal mind is vulnerable to intelligent investigative effort. The key word is effort. The effort begins with determining just what your objectives are for conducting surveillance in the first place. Foremost should be to obtain evidence of a crime.

Surveillance is a way to find an individual by watching his or her associates and friends. When seeking detailed data about a person's activities, there is no better method. Frequently, surveillance is necessary to locate stolen property or illegal activities.

Conducting surveillance provides the opportunity for public or private enforcement people to have the information necessary to conduct effective interrogation and to verify information received from other sources. These are two critical prerequisites for good surveillance. The first is to obtain admissible legal evidence for obtaining search warrants or testifying in court. The second and most obvious is to know at all times the whereabouts of an individual.

The principal attributes for a successful surveillance participant is that they possess patience and endurance. You must be alert and have the ability to act natural under all circumstances. A person should be resourceful, which includes the ability to look ordinary or nondescript in appearance, including your vehicle.

139

Surveillance of Premises

A surveillance of premises usually entails the use of a base of operation or a "plant," which is a room, apartment, store front, basement, loft warehouse, house, or some camouflaged outdoor fixture. A fixed plant should afford a maximum degree of observation and should have an exit to permit entry or exit without chance of observation from the object of the surveillance. This plant setup should be operated and maintained so that neighbors or occupants of the same location are not aware of or suspicious as to the existence or purpose of the operation.

If a fixed plant cannot be set up, than a camouflaged outdoor fixture such as a vendor's stand may be implemented. Hot dog or ice cream stands are very suitable for this purpose. Newspaper, magazine, and sundries may be used in lobby buildings. Cable television, line repair or installation allow for frequent motion and repositioning which might be necessary. They also allow for elevated "boom" or gantry work which under certain circumstances could be necessary.

When making observations from a plant you obviously do not want to be observed, so peering from windows is not recommended. However, the best coverage for such observations is venetian blinds. If venetian blinds would be out of place, it might be necessary to lower the draw shades an inch or more from the top to allow for observation. The use of binoculars, night-vision equipment, as well as camcorders and snooper-scopes may all be helpful in allowing legal advantages for a fixed surveillance.

When recording observations, you must not be selective in what you write or record. You must include everything that you observe. The unimportant has a unique way of becoming very important. You must record your observations, not what others may tell you they observed. The use of a chronological log is usually the best method of recording. The pertinent events, observations, and occurrences must be sufficiently detailed so as to be unmistakable in what was observed. Although you are under a degree of stress while attempting to record under difficult conditions, it is important that your observations are recorded in a timely manner. These observations should be in sufficient detail to enable you to recall them completely.

140

Surveillance Preparation

Study all available data relating to names, aliases, complete physical description, identifying characteristics and mannerisms. Know who the friends, associates, and contacts are. Obtain as many photos as possible. Learn all that is available about normal activities and habits. If it can be determined, you should know the person's propensity for violence and what, if any, criminal history they have. If it can be determined, it is helpful to know if the subject or object of your efforts is sensitive to or "tail conscious."

It is important to understand fully the neighborhood in which a surveillance is conducted: who are the inhabitants, what is the style of dress, what language or dialects are spoken? What should be your dress in order to match that of the locals? What types of vehicles are common to the area? Determine what vehicle license plates should be usual to the area. What the subject's driving habits? Where does he/she usually go? This is important to know in case the subject is "lost" in traffic; you can then check the known usual locations in order to reestablish contact. It is recommended that a reconnaissance be undertaken to learn the geography, look for suitable vantage points, obtain a feel for the traffic conditions, and learn the streets. The most embarrassing thing you can do is follow someone down a dead end street.

Always carry sufficient money to defray expenses. If you know that someone is likely to frequent expensive restaurants to meet others, be prepared. There are two suggestions that must be followed to be successful under these circumstances; it is wise to pay your check before your subject does so you can leave quickly, and when possible, you should leave before the subject does and reposition yourself outside.

141

Surveillance: Subjects' Methods of Detecting

It is quite natural for a "good guy," the one doing the surveillance, to assume or be convinced that he/she has been observed by the suspect(s). The tendency to become "hyper" under the tension of a surveillance is to be expected. Remain calm but be aware of the various methods and tricks that a suspect may employ to verify any suspicion of being under surveillance. Some of these are:

- Suspect stops abruptly and looks at people behind
- Head constantly looking or turning in all directions
- Reversing course and retracing steps
- Boarding transportation of any sort and leaving just before it starts to move
- Same as above only riding a short distance before leaving
- Circling the block in a taxi
- Taking the last taxi at a taxi stand
- Entering a building and leaving just as quickly via another exit
- Turning a corner and then stopping

- Dropping or placing something and watching to see if anyone picks the object up
- Varying the walking gate
- Stopping to adjust clothing
- Starting to leave a lobby or waiting room, then stopping suddenly to see if anyone gets up quickly without reason
- When in a hotel, the suspect may open or close the door and not actually leave, then look to see if anyone leaves
- Entering into crowds
- Entering a theater, club, amusement center, or something similar, than leaving through another entrance or exiting quickly
- Changing clothes while in motion
- Pointing you out to a policeman
- Suspect will drive his/her car to a parking lot and sit
- Suspect will drive to a parking lot and be picked up or change cars
- Suspect will have himself/herself followed in another car at a distance while communicating via cell phone
- Suspect, when driving, will drive fast, slow, and even down one-way streets
- Pulling into driveways
- Driving down dead end streets
- Making illegal u-turns or cross medians
- Running red lights
- Stopping suddenly around curves or corners

142

Surveillance: Use of Automobiles

It is obvious that when using a vehicle in a surveillance it must not be conspicuous or out of place for the conditions. It is just as obvious that when using a single car in a surveillance, it must be behind the subject vehicle with the distance varying with the amount of traffic. In city traffic, no more than two vehicles should be permitted to come between the subject vehicle and the surveillance vehicle.

In order to avoid the line of sight as much as possible of the subject's rear-view mirror, it is wise to position the surveillance vehicle to the right rear of the subject car. In rural areas and on highways, it is wise to give the subject vehicle a good lead. If intersections and forks in the road are few, you could extend the lead to a point where the subject may even be out of sight over hills or around curves. If at all possible, keep another vehicle between you and the subject.

In a two car surveillance, especially during daylight, both vehicles should be behind the subject. Occasionally, one car might operate on a known parallel route. If possible, the parallel car should time itself to arrive at intersections just before the subject vehicle. This is an especially effective method at night and in urban conditions. You should never use your high beams. On those rare occasions that three cars are used with a surveillance, the parallel method can be very effective; one vehicle can lead the subject and more closely observe the subject.

It is generally not good to conduct a vehicle surveillance alone. Usually two people are necessary—one to drive, the other to record and concentrate on the subject. It is wise to change seating if possible, front to back or simply check out of the line of sight of the subject if you are the passenger. Sometimes it is advisable to carry a woman's or man's hat or anything that can change the appearance of the passenger or driver. It is advisable to consider your own comfort during a vehicle surveillance. The simple things like food and drink can be placed in a bag beforehand. You should dress comfortably but appropriately, the latter in case you have to move out and about to place the subject in or at a particular location in the event that he or she leaves the vehicle. Remember to attend to you own personal body functions whenever the opportunity is possible. Surveillance can be stressful and long in duration.

143

Telemarketing Fraud and Protection[94]

In order to investigate this type of fraud, we suggest you understand how it can be prevented and what advice you would give a victim. "Your best protection is to just hang up the phone. If you think it is rude, tell them politely that you are not interested, don't want to waste their time, and please don't call back—and then hang up." If you find yourself caught up in a sales pitch, remember the federal government's Telemarketing Sales Rules:

- You have to be told the name of the company, the fact that it is a sales call, and what's being sold. If a prize is being offered, you have to be told immediately that there is no purchase necessary to win.
- If the caller says you have won a prize, you cannot be asked to pay anything for it. You cannot be required to pay shipping charges. If it is a sweepstakes, the caller must tell you how to enter without making a purchase.
- You cannot be asked to pay in advance for services such as repairing your credit record, finding a loan, or acquiring a prize they say you have won. You pay for services only if they are actually delivered.
- You shouldn't be called before 8:00 AM or after 9:00 PM. If you tell telemarketers not to call again, they cannot. If they do, they have broken the law.
- If you're guaranteed a refund, the caller has to tell you all the limitations.

And remember, don't give telemarketers your credit card number, your bank account number, or social security number. Don't authorize bank drafts—ever. If you suspect fraud, call the National Fraud Information Center at (800) 876-7060.

144

Telephone Use and Pretexting: Your Most Powerful Tool[95]

When searching for missing persons, the telephone is one of your most important tools. The telephone is to a researcher what a camera is to a photographer. Without the telephone, the researcher is out of business. This tool offers immediate, direct contact with an expert—commonly known as a human intelligence (HUMINT) source. But how do you get this information source to be forthcoming? Here, it is crucial that you develop a credible message that will evoke help from the authorities—providing them with the motivation to share information.

There are two basic approaches for this; the first is the *plain truth* (i.e., "I am a friend of the subject and am looking for him since we have not spoken since school"); the second approach is called *pretexting*. The plain truth is easy to understand, but what about pretexting? Some call it *pretending* and, admittedly, that pretty much says it. Pretexting is the development of a story designed to motivate an expert to provide the information necessary to locate the individual. In the investigative business, potential sources can either be sympathetic to our efforts, or not. By relying on a courteous approach, thoughtful questions, and employing some degree of natural charm, our goal here is to create a comfortable situation where our source will not be placed on the defensive. Remember, this expert is rarely required to talk with us, so to ingratiate ourselves we will need to put on our best face. To do this takes practice. And it also takes a *stratagem*, or a ruse.

THE STRATAGEM

Using your imagination, anticipate and plan for the conversation. Ensure that your story is credible. Ask yourself, why would someone be calling and asking for information? The most believable story is the obvious one: you are tracking down a long-lost friend from college, updating alumni information, or organizing a reunion. Or you are calling from a company verifying employment information prior to hiring, and so on. Is this legal? As long as you do not pretext as a known company when, in fact, you are not conducting that company's business, you are on pretty safe ground.

Practice what you are going to say, and practice being a professional—as if you are routinely verify information on people for a living. Be yourself and attempt to put the other person at ease. Remember, the expert is working at a job like most of us and is most likely just interested in doing a good job. After you are comfortable with your pretext, consider first calling the individual or expert who knows the most. Make the calls, and write down all the results on the dossier sheet form provided. Your search is then launched.

THE RULES FOR PRETEXTING

The general rules here are to *ask bright, clear, and concise questions.* Concise questions provide easily understandable information in the same sentence that ends with the question. It gives the expert enough information to volunteer further information that is then helpful to you. If you don't bring some information to the table, your expert might become defensive and unwilling to divulge critical information. Clear questions means that you must ask the question understandably. In other words, ask and ye shall receive an answer! You must actually ask the question, or the listener will not clearly understand that he or she is expected to respond. The listener is expected to volunteer information, and the expert does so because you have provided enough background information to enlist them in your cause.

What you should *not* do is ask obscure questions no one can understand or attempt to throw your weight around. Being domineering and pushy will get you nothing—except someone on the other end of the telephone hanging up. If someone says they don't feel comfortable talking with you, thank them immediately and acknowledge their concerns, but then ask just one more question prior to hanging up. But always be polite (the world has enough aggressive telephone cranks).

145

Testifying in Courtrooms[96]

At times you may be required to testify in court as a result of some incident at work. Below are some helpful hints to assist you.

- Being nervous is nothing new. Lawyers are even nervous. Go to court early before you are to testify.
- Observe where everyone is sitting and where you testify. At this point do not talk, laugh or whisper or cause any disturbance.
- When called upon, smile and make eye contact with the jurors when you answer the lawyer's questions.
- Remember, it's the jury not the judge that is going to decide on the outcome of the case.
- If you can, leave after you testify.
- Be aware of the fact that the jury may observe your behavior in the hallway and elevator.
- Finally, remember these six points:
  1. Tell the truth and do not exaggerate.
  2. Look the jurors in the eye; making eye contact is important.
  3. Lawyers ask questions, you answer to the jury.
  4. Give full and complete answers.
  5. During cross-examination, give short, truthful answers.
  6. Sit comfortably in the witness chair and avoid hand motion. Try locking your fingers together as if in prayer.

146

Totality of Circumstances Test[97]

Under the *totality of circumstances test*, judges are given considerable discretion in determining if a search warrant should be used. In *Gates*, however, it did not give the issuing judge unrestricted discretion to determine probable cause. In *Gates*, the Court wrote that "an affidavit must provide the issuing judge with a substantial basis for determining the existence of probable cause" (103 S.Ct. at 2332). In addition, the Court required that "sufficient information must be presented to the judge to allow that official to determine probable cause; his action cannot be a mere ratification of the conclusions of others. In order to ensure that such an abdication of the judge's duty does not occur, courts must continue to conscientiously review the sufficiency of affidavits on which warrants are issued" (103 S.Ct. at 2333).

147

Truck Tails[98]

Generally speaking, truck tails are much easier than automobile tails, and in corporate security work, they are probably more prevalent. Because of their size and unusual markings, trucks are easier to keep in sight than automobiles.

One thing that investigators must be aware of is that truck drivers rely on their large side-view mirrors. When making a turn, the tail car should always make a much wider turn than normal to keep out of view of the driver. On the other hand, because side-view mirrors represent the truck driver's only means of viewing to the rear, they are also an advantage. There is a blind spot immediately behind the truck, out of view of both side-view mirrors. To take advantage of this blind spot, the investigator must tailgate the truck, and a high degree of driver skill is required to avoid an accident. However, in heavy downtown traffic, this technique often represents the only way to stay with the truck at various intersections and through traffic signals.

In corporate security work, most truck surveillances are of company trucks that make regular deliveries or pick ups. Because these trucks generally follow a prescribed route, it is often possible to determine beforehand which stops the driver will make. The surveillance agent can make a dry run of the route in advance to study traffic conditions, special turns, bridges, and turnoffs. The dry run also provides an opportunity to spot various locations along the route that can be used to minimize the agent's exposure to a burn.

148

Undercover Investigations[99]

DRUGS

In recent years, the use of narcotics and dangerous drugs has affected virtually every company in the United States to some degree. Experience has shown that the use of drugs, including marijuana, has an adverse effect on both the worker and the company. Worker's compensation cases costing tens of thousands of dollars sometimes arise in plants that have problems with illegal drug use. Absenteeism, tardiness, and employee mistakes are another result of drug use. Generally, whenever large-scale gambling or illicit traffic in drugs is prevalent in an industrial plant, it is accompanied by the theft of company property.

Many firms have instituted preemployment drug screening. However, without a policy of random on-the-job testing, such preemployment programs have little impact. The body purges itself within 30 days of any drug residues that are normally picked up by a urinalysis. A few companies use a saliva cream (the "spit test") to detect the smoking of marijuana during breaks and lunch periods. This test, developed by UCLA scientists, is valid for a four-hour period after smoking. However, its use has not caught on in U.S. industry. Obviously, a complete approach to the problem of on-the-job drug use might include the use of undercover agents.

Many drugs are dispensed on company property in glassine envelopes or plastic bags. Marijuana cigarettes, or "joints," are frequently contained in regular cigarette packages, such as flip-top boxes. Marijuana cigarettes are occasionally disguised with legitimate cigarette papers and filters. The tobacco is removed from a filter-tip cigarette and replaced with marijuana. The only obvious difference is that the end of the cigarette paper is twisted to prevent the marijuana from escaping. When placed filter-tip up in a normal cigarette package, the marijuana cigarettes are difficult to distinguish from regular cigarettes.

The most common drugs found in industrial plants and private companies today are marijuana, hashish (hash), and methamphetamine (speed). As a rule, the harder drugs—heroin, morphine, and cocaine—are usually not present in great quantity. These drugs adversely affect the worker's performance to the extent that their use would be obvious to even the most inexperienced observer. Workers who use drugs generally lean toward stimulants from the amphetamine family or hallucinogens like marijuana or hashish. The use of LSD in the workplace is rare.

GLOSSARY OF TERMS

The Drug Enforcement Administration (DEA) provides the following glossary of slang terms for drugs. Many of these terms are commonly heard in the private employment sector.

Amphetamines: Beans, bennies, black beauties, black mollies, copilots, crank, crossroads, crystal dexies, double cross, meth, minibennies, pep pills, rosas, roses, speed, thru truck drivers, uppers, wake-ups, whites

Barbiturates: Barbs, blockbusters, bluebirds, blue devils, blues, Christmas trees, downers, green dragons, Mexican reds, nebbies, nimbies, pajaro rojo, pink ladies, pinks, rainbows, reds, red and blues, redbirds, red devils, sleeping pills, stumblers, yellow jackets, yellows

Cocaine: Blow, C, coca, coke, crack, dust, flake, girl, heaven, lady, mujer, nose candy, paradise, perico, polvo blanco, rock, snow, white

Hashish: Goma do mota, hash, soles

Heroin: Big H, boy, brown, brown sugar, caballo, chiva, crap, estuffa, H, heronia, hombre, horse, junk, Mexican mud, polvo, scag, smack, stuff, thing

LSD: Acid, blotter acid, California sunshine, haze, microdots, paper acid, purple haze, sunshine, wedges, window panes

Marijuana: Acapulco gold, cannabis, Colombian, ganga, grass, griffa, hemp, herb, J, jay, joint, Mary Lane, mota, mutah, Panama red, pot, reefer, sativa, smoke, stick, tea, weed, yerba

Peyote: Buttons, cactus, mesc, mescal, mescal buttons

Methaqualone: Quaalude, quads, guas, soapers, so pes, sopor

Morphine: Cube, first line, goma, morf, morfina, morpho, morphy, mud

Phencyclidine: Angel dust, crystal, cyclkone, hog, PCP, peace pill, rocket fuel, supergrass, tic tac

UNDERCOVER AGENTS

Undercover agents must know the slang terms currently used for various illegal drugs in their locale. In addition, they should recognize illegal drugs when they encounter them and should be able to make "buys," preserving the drugs for future evidence.

If drugs are present in the workplace, the undercover agent's prime objective is to gather evidence of drug traffic and use. This is normally done by making buys. The agent should have no difficulty buying a joint of marijuana or some capsules of speed. Any drugs purchased should be preserved for evidence and later used in an interrogation.

Certain legal considerations must be taken into account when making buys or even possessing illicit drug contraband. In the state of Georgia, for example, it is against the law to purchase illegal drugs. In other states, you can be arrested for possession of an illegal substance. New agents must understand what can go wrong if they are caught up in these circumstances. For example, an auto accident on the way home from work on the day of a "buy" might very well land the agent in jail. The agent's handler can probably intercede with the police to sidetrack any prosecution, but in the process there is a great likelihood that the agent's cover will be blown.

The only practical approach is for the agent's supervisors to arrange a clearance for such activity with the proper police authority. Traditionally, the police have exhibited little interest in use of minor amounts of marijuana in the industrial setting. They are usually content to let the operative proceed without any further police involvement and allow the case to be closed by the company's own security manager.

However, sales within the company of cocaine, other hard drugs, or large amounts of marijuana are a different matter. When the police do not have sufficient human resources to send in their own in-plant operative, they will usually allow the undercover person to act as their own agent. Some police officials will want the agent to immediately turn in to them any "buys" made in the plant. Others will accept the agent's marking and preservation of the drug contraband and even permit the agent to hold the evidence until the end of the case.

If good police relations have been established, the company security manager may be able to conclude the theft portion of the case at the same time the police close up the drug facet. In this way, neither party's case will be affected by premature action on the other's part.

The biggest problem encountered by undercover agents today will be in participating with suspected employees in social gatherings where marijuana or hash are regularly used. A number of agents claim that they can simulate taking a "drag" on a joint as it is passed around in such a group. The experience of most legitimate undercover operatives shows that an agent is seldom accepted by a pot-smoking group unless the group believes that the agent is a marijuana user; the group will not accept someone who they think is "straight." Once rejected, it may become impossible for the agent to gather physical evidence of marijuana use. This creates a dilemma for the security director: should the agent be allowed to participate if he or she is not able to successfully simulate the act of marijuana smoking? There is no easy answer for this and each security manager will have to make an individual decision.

Many agents also claim that they can feign euphoria or simulate heightened physical activity as a result of taking a "hit" of speed. The problem with these activities is that when the agent is cross-examined in court, prior drug use is almost always brought up to impeach or discredit the agent's testimony. Agents who make good witnesses are often able to convince arbitrators or judges that they did not, in fact, take drugs and only simulated their use. On the other hand, there are many successful agents who have had no prior experience with drugs, including marijuana, yet were able to infiltrate social groups without using or feigning the use of drugs.

Professional security administrators certainly do not want their security agents to become drug users, nor do they want to see the agents' court testimony impeached or discredited. On the other hand, agents are faced with the task of infiltrating employee groups that see nothing wrong with the social use of softer drugs. Without question, this presents a very delicate problem in formulating policy.

MARKING EVIDENCE

Undercover agents sometimes need to mark caches of merchandise hidden on company property, awaiting removal in a theft case. An ideal method of marking such property is with a florescent crayon, but adequate markings can also be made with an ordinary ballpoint pen without compromising the investigation.

When an agent marks for future evidence a cache of stolen merchandise or other company property, the agent's daily report should reflect exactly when it was marked, the manner in which it was marked, and where the distinguishing marks were placed. By carefully describing how the evidence was marked, it is possible to have a completely tight presentation of physical evidence at a subsequent trial, arbitration, or other proceeding. Likewise, with the recovery of any physical evidence of gambling and drugs, the details of the recovery and marking of evidence must be reported completely in the daily report. It is often possible to recover stolen property that the undercover agent has marked, and this later becomes the basis of a specific criminal complaint for larceny. Sometimes an undercover agent, working with another investigator assigned to outside surveillance, is able to recover evidence of property that is in the process of being stolen.

STAGING

In his book, *The Spymasters of Israel*, Stewart Steven (1980), described the staging of Eli Cohen, Israel's greatest spy. To prepare Cohen for eventual infiltration into Syria, his controllers worked out a cover story that closely matched Cohen's own background. The cover included the fact that he had been born in Beirut, Lebanon, to Syrian parents. The family had purportedly emigrated to Alexandria, Egypt, and had then gone on to Buenos Aires, Argentina. Steven reports that at the time of staging, there were more than half a million Arabs living in Buenos Aires, many of whom were Syrian. Cohen successfully completed his staging within nine months of his arrival in Argentina. His next step was the penetration itself—Damascus.

When operating a nationwide undercover program, security executives occasionally run into assignments that tax their ingenuity. Such a case occurred in an undercover job in Jackson, Mississippi. There were no southern investigators on the staff who were available for this assignment, and it fell to an investigator from one of the western states. Because Jackson is not the type of city to which people drift from other parts of the United States, extra attention was given to the agent's staging. The following paragraphs describe the steps taken to establish a cover and staging for the assignment.

The undercover agent was first sent to New Orleans, where he spent enough time to become acquainted with the city. From New Orleans, he moved to Jackson. His cover story was that he had gone to New Orleans to see if he could get an athletic scholarship at a local university. After he was turned down, someone suggested that he apply for the same type of scholarship at the local university in Jackson, which also turned him down because of poor grades.

The agent established the usual local cover by obtaining a Mississippi driver's license and Mississippi license plates. He spent many days at the public library reading back copies of the Jackson newspaper to become familiar with the local events of the last six months. He found a job in a drive-in restaurant, where he worked for a number of months. The agent used this job as an employment reference for obtaining work at his assigned location. Even though he obviously spoke with a western accent rather than a southern drawl, his story of attempting schooling in New Orleans and in Jackson was accepted, and, ultimately, so was the investigator.

149

Understanding Financial Paper Flow

Investigators are often called upon to provide a due diligence report on some business or another. More often than not, the assignment appears to be overwhelming due in part to a lack of knowledge or experience on where to begin to understand two important end documents concerning any company or organization: the balance sheet and the income statement. We have broken down the process into three specific areas and these are records, explanations, and general summaries. The contributing documents for each are outlined below. They should make the process easier to understand and to follow.

Records include:

- Checks and cash authorizations
- Sales invoices
- Deposits of cash
- Financial adjustments/corrections
- Payables for operating or administrative expenses

Journals include:

- Cash disbursement journals
- Sales journal
- Purchases journal
- Cash receipts journal
- General operating journal

Ledgers include:

- Assets
- Liabilities
- Capital
- Income
- Expenses

All of the ledgers flow into either the income statement or the balance sheet, income and expenses into the income statement and assets, liabilities, and capital into the balance sheet. These are the sources of all the numbers that flow into how the value of any company or organization is organized, whether the transactions are processed the old-fashioned way or electronically via software programs. Keep it simple.

150

Vehicle Searches[100]

The authority to conduct a warrantless search of a motor vehicle is one of the oldest yet most misunderstood exceptions to the warrant requirement. In *Carroll v. U.S.*, the Court held that peace officers may search a vehicle if three factors are present. First, the officers must have probable cause to believe that evidence of a crime or contraband is concealed somewhere in the vehicle. Second, the vehicle must be in a place where it is lawfully accessible to the police, such as on a city street. Finally, the scope of the search must be restricted to areas where the item searched for could be hidden. For example, police could not search for a stolen engine in a glove compartment (*Carroll v. United States*, 267 U.S. 132 (1925)).

In 1982, the Supreme Court expanded this vehicle exception in *United States v. Ross*. In this case, police had information from a reliable informant that Ross had heroin in the trunk of his car. The informant described Ross, his automobile, and where his transactions took place in detail. Officers proceeded to the location and saw a man matching Ross's description. Ross was arrested and his car was searched. Officers found a gun and ammunition in the glove compartment. Officers then opened the trunk with Ross's keys, where they found a closed brown paper bag containing a substance later identified as heroin. They also found a leather pouch containing approximately $3,200. The Court held that when police have probable cause to believe that a vehicle contains the fruits or instrumentalities of a crime or contraband, they may search the entire vehicle, including any areas that might contain the item they seek (*United States v. Ross*, 456 U.S. 798 (1982)). Unlike searches incident to arrest, vehicle searches need not be conducted at the time the vehicle is seized (*Chambers v. Maroney*, 399 U.S. 42 (1970)). Recreational vehicles and campers are subject to the vehicle exception as long as they are mobile and in an area accessible to the police (*California v. Carney*, 471 U.S. 386 (1985)).

VEHICLE SEARCHES, INVENTORY, AND IMPOUND[101]

Law enforcement officers are often required to take possession of a motor vehicle to protect the interests of the department, the individual officer, and the owner of the vehicle. When police impound a vehicle, they assume the role of *involuntary bailee*, that is, they have a limited obligation to see that the vehicle or property is placed in a location where it will be secure. Once the vehicle is impounded, police must inventory its contents to determine the presence of valuables or dangerous items. If, while conducting the inventory, police find contraband, the item may be seized and the owner prosecuted for possessing it (*South Dakota v. Opperman*, 428 U.S. 364 (1976)). Inventory searches are valid if:

1. The officer is legally in possession of the vehicle, such as impounding an illegally parked car.
2. The officer is acting pursuant to a standard department operational procedure.
3. The police are not acting in bad faith, or for the sole purpose of conducting an investigation to discover incriminating evidence (*Colorado v. Bertine*, 479 U.S. 564 (1987); *Florida v. Wells*, 110 S.Ct. 1621 (1990)).

WARRANTLESS SEARCH OF THE PERSON INCIDENT TO ARREST

The Search for Weapons

Because a search of the person incident to arrest for weapons is an intrusion of privacy, the Fourth Amendment and many state laws require that it be reasonable. In order for it to be reasonable, it is not enough to speculate that any person *might* have a small weapon concealed on his person because of your past experience in finding razorblades or needles hidden in shoes, lapels, hatbands, coat linings, or attached to the body. You should have reason to suspect that *this* particular arrestee may have such weapons so concealed in order to justify more than an ordinary search for a weapon the size of a gun, knife, or club.

Your experience is a major guide in deciding how extensively you should search the person for weapons. The following factors may be relevant:

1. Your pat-down or your evidence search turned up a weapon, indicating that the person was potentially violent.
2. Based on your perceptions as an experienced police officer, the person's behavior on being arrested was abnormal; for instance, he was unnaturally resistant or unnaturally calm, or he said something odd.
3. Your know from personal experience, from others, or from records that the person is known to carry weapons or to be violent.
4. The offense for which you made the arrest involved weapons.
5. The offense for which you made the arrest is one that frequently involves people with weapons, such as prostitution or narcotics.
6. The place you searched was one from which the suspect could have taken a weapon in the custodial situation.

These are factors you should consider in deciding where to search for weapons and this analysis will promote the admissibility of any evidence you seize, whether relating to the arrest crime or to another crime.

Any article that is locked or sealed may be taken from the suspect, but it should not be opened to search for weapons (unless you have reason to suspect it contains an explosive device), because the suspect could not have taken a weapon from it while he held it and you are protected by removing the article from the suspect's possession.

Plain View

The rationale for the "plain view" doctrine is simply that when an officer in the course of his duties inadvertently comes across incriminating evidence he should have the power to seize it immediately without going through the inconvenience and possible danger of securing a search warrant. In order to keep the doctrine from swallowing up the rule of preference for warrants, the court has put two significant restraints on when an object validly may be seized under the doctrine.

First, the discovery must be inadvertent or accidental. If the initial intrusion is bottomed upon a warrant which fails to mention a particular object, though the police know its location and intend to seize it, then there is a violation of the express requirement of "warrants . . . particularly describing [the] things to be seized" *Coolidge v. New Hampshire*, 403 U.S. 443 (1971). In addition, if the discovery is not inadvertent, then the rationale of the rule fails because "the inconvenience of procurring a warrant to cover an inadvertent discovery . . ." is no longer present.

The second factor that must be present for a valid search under the plain view doctrine is that there is a "prior justification for an intrusion" *Coolidge v. New Hampshire, id*; see also *Ker v. California*, 374 U.S. 23 (1963).

It is reasoned that the plain view doctrine will not extend these situations if limited to those in which a prior justification already exists. Therefore, the guidelines support and the law upholds a plain view search and seizure only where the intrusion suffered was initiated during the valid exercise of police duties and not for the purpose of getting a "plain view" of incriminating evidence.

The Search for Evidence

Because a search of the person for evidence is an intrusion of privacy, the Fourth Amendment requires that the search be reasonable. When you have reason to suspect that the arrestee possesses evidence, under the Massachusetts law, the evidence search will be reasonable if:

1. The search is for evidence of the crime for which the arrest is made, and
2. The size of the evidence is such that it could be contained in the places where you search.

If an article is locked or sealed, you may take it from the arrestee. If you wish to search it for evidence, it is preferable that you try to obtain a search warrant.

Here is an example case. You arrest William Boyce on a warrant for receiving stolen property: six men's wrist watches. You believe he has the watches on his person. You search his right coat pocket and find two watches matching the description of the stolen watches. You search his left coat pocket and find there three gold bracelets, all with initials different from his. You may seize them, too, as the initials plus the fact that there are three of them give you probable cause to believe they are stolen. If they prove to be stolen, they may be used as evidence on a second receiving charge. In his inside coat pocket, you find a box 6 × 4 × 2 inches that is taped shut. You take the box. The fact that there still are four watches you have not found plus the size of the box gives you probable cause to believe the box may contain the missing watches. Using those facts, you may open the box. It is preferable, however, for you to apply for a search warrant before cutting the tape on the box and opening it, because the sealing indicates a high expectation of privacy. When you open the box, you find that it contains 60 decks of heroin. The fact that they were discovered accidentally during a search with a warrant will help assure their admissibility as evidence on a possession with intent to sell charge.

CAR SEARCH CHECKLIST

1. Examination of auto interior or exterior without entry
   a. Purpose: What does officer expect to find?
   b. Cause: Why is particular auto singled out?
   c. Result: What is found? What subsequent action?
   d. Authority: Does officer have doubt about his authority to do what he did?
   e. Situations in which above examination might have been useful but was not done.
2. Arrest of vehicle occupant
   a. Where is driver when vehicle is searched?
   b. If vehicle is not searched, why?
   c. Do officers fear weapons? Why?
   d. Do officers tailor scope of the search to the crime?
   e. How do crowd and traffic conditions affect the search?
3. Noncustody vehicle stop
   a. For traffic offense or for investigation?
   b. Weapons search? Why?
   c. Passengers searched or frisked?
4. Extensive searches
   a. Probable cause?
   b. How long does search take?
   c. How thorough is search?
   d. Is car towed for subsequent search? For impoundment?
   e. Is passenger searched? Before or after car and driver?
5. Consent searches
   a. How does officer ask for consent? What does he say? Whom does he ask?
   b. Is consent a necessity or a courtesy?
   c. Can you identify why an officer chooses NOT to conduct a consent search?
6. Probable cause search of vehicle not in use
   a. Do officers discuss possibility of warrant?

  b. Is attempt made to evaluate mobility of vehicle?
  c. Is consideration given to possibility of access to vehicle by others?
7. Finally, what do your department's policies and procedures say regarding car search and inventory of vehicle before towing?

Appendix A

Things Are Not Always As They Appear

By Patrick J. Lenaghan, CPP[102]

While investigating a fatal traffic accident (which had no eye witnesses other than the driver), it became obvious that things are not always as they appear on a police report. At 9:05 PM on a dark February night, a 35-year-old female was ejected from a rural tavern located along a secondary blacktop road. While walking, she was struck by a car and killed. Two state highway patrolmen responded. They conducted a cursory investigation and charged the driver with misdemeanor death by vehicle and careless and reckless operation of a vehicle. Up to this point, the actions of the two highway patrolmen were appropriate (death by vehicle is a misdemeanor unless alcohol is involved).

The accident reported stated the following:

> Vehicle #1 was travelling southeast on Rural Road One and entered into a gradual left hand curve at an excessive rate of speed (estimated at 80 MPH). Vehicle #1 ran off the road onto the right shoulder, traveled 82.8 feet and struck a victim who was walking southeast on the right shoulder of the road. After impact with the victim, vehicle #1 continued travelling 224 feet on the right shoulder area, before reentering Rural Road One. Vehicle #1 traveled 101 feet across Rural Road One and ran into the left drainage ditch. After the impact into left drainage ditch, vehicle #1 traveled 44 feet and came to a stop in the drainage ditch facing south. Upon impact with Vehicle #1, the victim penetrated the windshield of the vehicle and became lodged and remained in the windshield until the vehicle came to a stop in the drainage ditch. Emergency personnel had to extract the victim from the windshield and the interior of vehicle #1.

The subsequent accident investigation by the same officers supported their initial report.

The driver of vehicle #1 stated to the best of his recollection that:

> "I was driving down (south) on Rural Road One at about 50 MPH (the speed limit is 45 MPH). When I took the curve by the tavern, I saw what I thought was a hand. I jerked the wheel to the left. Then something came through the windshield. I then jerked the wheel to the right and went off the road onto the (west) shoulder of the road. I knew that I had hit something and when I looked over to the passenger side of the car, I had a body stuck in my windshield. I

freaked out. I then jerked the wheel to the left. The car went across the road (east) and came to a stop in the drainage ditch. Sometime while I was braking, I got out of the car—I guess through the window.

On initial review, the police report would seem to be more logical and closer to the actual events than the driver's recollection. However, at stake here was a prison term of one year if the driver was convicted—not to mention civil litigation by the victim's family.

While conducting this investigation, we employed ten tenets or techniques that proved useful. The following tenets are not in any particular order, and several were employed simultaneously to save time.

1. Don't accept the police report on face value just because you assume that they are trained professionals. Do your own investigation.
2. Work with the client to get a concise and detailed account of the events as they happened and as accurately as possible.
3. Exam closely and photograph the vehicle as soon as possible. Photograph it from all angles and sides—especially for damage. Try to have the driver present.
4. Interview the medical, emergency personnel, and bystanders who were at the scene.
5. Attempt to reenact as much of the accident as you can within safety limitations. Use computer simulations.
6. Consider the overall accident scene and the surrounding area—don't just concentrate on the roadway and shoulder area.
7. The toxicology and the medical examiner's reports are important to any investigation.
8. Interview other policemen as to their experiences with accidents under similar circumstances.
9. Conduct your own investigation of the events that led up to the accident—include a background investigation of the victim and your client.
10. When consulting with experts, use several (it is helpful if they are not associates).

DON'T ACCEPT THE POLICE REPORT ON FACE VALUE

We were called into the case approximately two weeks after the accident took place and immediately went to the scene. Utilizing the police accident report and paint and skid marks still visible on the road, we were able to reconstruct their investigation. From these sources, we verified the police measurements and made our own. We videotaped and photographed all aspects of our investigation for future use. Another technique we used was to videotape and photograph the surrounding area. Videotape is invaluable later as you work on the case in the office. It allows you to revisit the accident scene whenever you have a question without having to go back to the actual scene. In our case, it was over 100 miles away.

EXAMINE AND PHOTOGRAPH THE VEHICLE FROM
ALL SIDES AND ANGLES

Examine and photograph the vehicle as soon as possible. This is vital. In our case, the vehicle was compacted (crushed) by order of the insurance company only two days after we examined it. It is also helpful to have the owner with you so that he can point out what damage was caused by the accident and what was done previously. Take pictures from all angles and sides. Photograph all the damage in detail (in this case, we were able to find blood and bone fragments which would serve as positive proof of the victim's point of impact). This technique was a key element in our case. Research all aspects of the car's performance and study the physical characteristics of the car, such as ground clearance and wheel base.

WORK WITH YOUR CLIENT TO GET A CONCISE VERSION AS TO
WHAT HAPPENED AS ACCURATELY AS POSSIBLE

It is critical to sit down with the client and debrief him in detail as to what actually happened. Take it slowly, step by step. Be patient and try to get as much detail as possible. In our case, the client had a slight learning disability and it was necessary to work slowly and help him reenact what happened. Remember that the driver has undergone a significant emotional event, and may have some difficulty articulating what actually happened.

INTERVIEW THE PARAMEDICS, EMERGENCY PERSONNEL, AND
ANY BYSTANDERS WHO WERE ON THE SCENE

Because the driver was the only witness, it was useful to interview the emergency personnel who responded to the accident. They were able to describe the condition of the driver, the scene, and most importantly, the condition of the victim. This was critical because at some point after impact, the victim's right leg was severed from the body. It was thrown clear of the vehicle and came to rest on the side of the road. The position of this limb would be key to the police investigation. They supposed the point of impact was in the vicinity of the severed limb. As a result of this, they flagrantly disregarded much of the other physical evidence available. The emergency personnel were also able to verify statements made by the driver (while in his agitated state) as to what happened. These remarks helped to validate his later statements when we interviewed him.

THE TOXICOLOGY AND THE MEDICAL EXAMINER'S
REPORT ARE IMPORTANT TO ANY INVESTIGATION

The medical examiner's report is usually unbiased and thorough. It provides invaluable information as to the damages sustained, and in this case this information was critical in establishing what really happened. From this report, we were able to match the injuries to the victim to the damage to the vehicle and establish the point of impact and speed of the vehicle. The toxicology report was also useful. The postmortem toxicology report determined that the deceased's blood alcohol level was 490 mg/dl and 510 mg/dl. Any higher, and the victim would have been approaching cardiac arrest.

REENACT THE ACCIDENT AND CIRCUMSTANCES WITHIN SAFETY LIMITATIONS

In driving the route as specified by the client, we found that it was difficult (if not impossible) to attain the speeds specified in the officers' report. The actual condition of the road and the physical layout of the road prohibited us (even in daylight) from attaining the speeds as cited in the report. The road is very twisted and has several slight hills, which forced us to maintain a reasonable speed. Also, the road condition in front of the tavern at the curve has a low shoulder. The tendency is to negotiate the curve more toward the center of the road and not the shoulder. Another technique we employed was to use computer simulations of the accident and the effects on the vehicle when it negotiated the curve at excessive speeds.

CONSIDER THE OVERALL ACCIDENT SCENE AND THE SURROUNDING AREA

At the top of the gradual left-hand turn was a washed out area approximately six inches deep that terminated in a gravel mound. The actual shoulder of the road was very narrow. It was on a slope (approximately 30 degrees) and bordered by a deep drainage ditch. The ditch on the east side of the road (where the vehicle finally stopped) had wide shoulders which caused the vehicle to become wedged and finally brought the vehicle to a stop. An evaluation of the surrounding area did not corroborate the police version of what happened when the driver took the turn. It also did not support their theory as to where the point of impact was on the roadway.

INTERVIEW OTHER POLICE OFFICERS ABOUT THEIR EXPERIENCE UNDER LIKE CIRCUMSTANCES

We interviewed several police traffic officers from other departments as to their experiences with single-vehicle fatal accidents. It is advisable to consult with officers out of state, and not local or state officers who may know the investigating officers. We also gave them this scenario and asked them their opinions as to what should have happened and the accuracy of the police investigation. All stated that the injuries and final disposition of the victim were not consistent with the rate of speed that the driver was alleged to have been driving. They were very helpful in providing additional information and leads as to what to look for.

WHEN CONSULTING WITH EXPERTS USE SEVERAL— PREFERABLY NOT ASSOCIATES

We consulted with two traffic reconstruction experts from two different states. These individuals were not associates but had similar credentials and experience. Both were given identical information packets to evaluate. Their results were almost identical and coincided with our theory as to what actually happened. By using experts from other states and not known to each other, the validity of the evaluation was much more credible in court.

CONDUCT YOUR OWN INVESTIGATIONS AS TO THE EVENTS THAT LEAD UP TO THE ACCIDENT

This should also include the backgrounds of the victim and the client. It may seem unusual to conduct your own investigation into the client's background, but this is a good practice to get into. It is helpful in establishing the client's credibility, past record, and whether he/she is telling the truth. In the case of the victim, it was very useful. It established that the victim was a habitual abuser of both alcohol and drugs and was also estranged from her husband and family. This would be helpful to the insurance company in a later litigation.

WHAT DID ACTUALLY HAPPEN?

Using the methods described above, we formulated the following theory of what actually happened. The driver (as he originally stated) was traveling at a speed of 50–53 MPH. As he entered the gradual left turn, his speed was well below the 80 MPH alleged by the highway patrol. We based that on the fact (from our interviews) that he was able to remember in great detail the activity in front of the tavern. It is obvious, therefore, that he had not out-run his headlights and had control of the vehicle.

He did not leave the roadway as the troopers maintained. The natural tendency for most drivers is to stay more to the center line when they go into a curve. This is especially true if they are familiar with the area, know that the parking area in front of the tavern is loose gravel and the shoulder is also very rough. We filmed several cars as they negotiated this curve and they all had a tendency to stay toward the center line as opposed to taking the curve wide. In investigating our client's background, we found out from a check of his previous driving record in another state, that he is legally blind in his right eye. It would, therefore, be natural for him to overcompensate and to drift more to the left than the right when negotiating the curve.

The condition of the area around where the troopers stated that the driver left the road did not support their theory as to the rate of speed he was alleged to have been traveling. If the driver had left the road at that point, the obstacles present at the washed out area would have had a dramatic effect on the post-accident condition of the vehicle. There was no damage consistent with this on the vehicle. At that speed, he would have encountered loose gravel and mud, which should have unnaturally affected his control of the vehicle, even if he had maintained control, he would have hit the gravel mound at a high rate of speed. The result of encountering all these obstacles at the alleged high rate of speed should have sent the vehicle off into a field along the side of the road or into the ditch. A computer reenactment showed that the vehicle would have rolled or come to rest on its side. This, of course, didn't happen. Also, after visiting the site and reviewing the videotapes, there was a lack of forensic evidence and the area was undisturbed.

The toxicology report showed that the victim (at the time of the accident) was well beyond legally drunk. In her condition, the victim could only have had limited motor coordination. After leaving the tavern, it was reported that the victim could hardly stand up and was staggering. It is logical, therefore, that in that condition, the victim would have taken the path of least resistance and was walking on the road and not the shoulder. To walk on the shoulder, as the troopers maintained, would have the victim trying to negotiate the sloping ground that provides drainage to the ditch along the side of the road. It would be very difficult for the victim to walk on that slope in that condition. It was also very dark that night and the uneven ground, trash, and debris along that stretch of the road would also force the victim to walk on the pavement.

Therefore, after passing the tavern and completing the curve, the driver encountered the victim in the road (as he stated). In the victim's condition, it was probable that there may have been impairment of hearing or any cogent association of the headlights with a vehicle approaching from the rear. Her reactions would be slowed or impaired, so she would not be cognizant of the danger. At the last second, she put her hand out (which was the driver's statement). She was struck by the vehicle (consistent with the damage to the vehicle and bone fragments) just to the left of the headlight, close to the center of the hood. She then skidded along the hood and entered the lower portion of the windshield.

Additionally, the distance from the point where the victim impacted the vehicle, supported by evidence of dents and bone fragments, to the outside fender was 28 feet. When we measured the width of the shoulder and compared it to where the troopers alleged that she was standing at the time of impact, based on the severed limb, we found that the right front tire would have been in the drainage ditch.

The position of the body also supported the claim of the driver that he was not driving at excessive speeds. Our research (having consulted with several traffic reconstruction experts and police officers) had shown that impact at the speed alleged by the troopers usually throws the body up and over the vehicle, tossing it as far as 200 feet. In this case, the victim slid along the hood and entered the driver's compartment low on the windshield, which is consistent with an impact between 50–60 MPH. Additionally, the damage to the windshield (the spiraling of the glass versus shattering) was also consistent with impact at lower speeds.

The driver maintained that he jerked the wheel to the left, crossing the road to the west side of the road. We feel that he jerked the wheel slightly to the left but did not cross the road (at that time), then jerked the wheel back to the right and ran down the side of the road on the right shoulder (his tracks are clearly visible in our photographs). The driver did not leave the road at the curve, travel 82.8 feet, and hit the victim on the shoulder of the road as stated by the highway patrol. The point of impact was further up the road and almost centered—not where the severed limb came to rest.

The driver, in his agitated state, stated that he had exited the vehicle through a window. It is much more likely that after his vehicle started to cross the road and he applied his brakes, he exited the vehicle via the door, rolling out of the vehicle and onto the grassy shoulder on the east side and not the roadway. When the vehicle entered the ditch, the sides of the ditch forced the door closed—when we examined the vehicle, mud was in the door hinge and along the side of the door.

CONCLUSION

When this evidence was presented at the trial, the driver was found innocent of all charges. During cross-examination of the troopers, it was learned that they had minimal training and limited experience in traffic accident investigations involving a fatality. Both officers were publicly admonished from the bench for their lack of thoroughness in conducting their investigation.

SO THINGS ARE NOT ALWAYS AS THEY APPEAR.

Notes

1. Michael F. Brown, *Criminal Investigations, Law and Practice* (Boston: Butterworth-Heinemann, 1998) http://www.bh.com.
2. Leonard Territo, James B. Halsted, and Max L. Bromley, *Crime and Justice in America: A Human Perspective*, 5th Ed. (Boston: Butterworth-Heineman, 1998) http://www.bh.com.
3. Ibid.
4. Permission to reproduce obtained from Chris Hertig, CPP, CPO, York College, Pennsylvania.
5. David A. Maxwell, J.D., CPP, *Private Security Law, Case Studies* (Boston: Butterworth-Heinemann, 1993) http://www.bh.com.
6. Michael F. Brown, *Criminal Investigations, Law and Practice* (Boston: Butterworth-Heinemann, 1998) http://www.bh.com.
7. Pursuant to Massachusetts General Laws, Chapter 266, Section 1.
8. Van Ritch, *Background Investigations* (Durham, N.C.: Carolina Academic Press, 1997) (www.cap.press.com).
9. Leonard Territo, James B. Halsted, and Max L. Bromley, *Crime and Justice in America: A Human Perspective*, 5th Ed. (Boston: Butterworth-Heinemann, 1998) http://www.bh.com.
10. Ibid.
11. J. Kirk Barefoot, *Undercover Investigations*, 3rd Ed. (Boston: Butterworth-Heinemann, 1995).
12. Philip P. Purpura, *Criminal Justice: An Introduction* (Boston: Butterworth-Heinemann, 1997).
13. Ibid.
14. Ibid.
15. Ibid.
16. Ibid.
17. Ibid.
18. J. Kirk Barefoot, *Undercover Investigations*, 3rd Ed. (Boston: Butterworth-Heinemann, 1995).
19. Michael F. Brown, *Criminal Investigations, Law and Practice* (Boston: Butterworth-Heinemann, 1998).
20. Philip P. Purpura, *Criminal Justice: An Introduction* (Boston: Butterworth-Heinemann, 1997).
21. Ibid.
22. Wesley Gilmer, *The Law Dictionary,* 6th Ed. (Cincinnati: Anderson Pub., 1986), pp. 265–266.
23. Philip P. Purpura, *Criminal Justice: An Introduction* (Boston: Butterworth-Heinemann, 1997).
24. Ibid.

25. Ibid.
26. Ibid.
27. Lydia Voigt et al., *Criminology and Justice* (New York: McGraw-Hill, 1994), pp. 47–48.
28. Wesley Gilmer, *The Law Dictionary*, 6th Ed. (Cincinnati: Anderson Pub., 1986), pp. 265–266.
29. Philip P. Purpura, *Modern Security and Loss Prevention Management* (Boston: Butterworth-Heinemann, 1989), pp. 298–299.
30. Philip P. Purpura, *Criminal Justice: An Introduction* (Boston: Butterworth-Heinemann, 1997).
31. David Popenoe, *Sociology*, 4th Ed. (Englewood Cliffs, NJ: Prentice-Hall, 1980), p. 111.
32. Barbara Boland et al., *The Prosecution of Felony Arrests*, 1988 (Washington, DC: Bureau of Justice Statistics, February 1992), p. 3.
33. U.S. Dept. of Justice, *Habitual Juvenile Offenders: Guidelines for Citizen Action and Public Response* (Washington, DC: Office of Juvenile Justice and Delinquency Prevention, October, 1991), p. 35.
34. Joseph F. Sheley, *Criminology*, 2nd Ed. (Belmont, CA: Wadsworth Pub., 1995), pp. 345–346.
35. Watson, pp. 13–14.
36. A. C. Germann et al., *Introduction to Law Enforcement and Criminal Justice* (Springfield, IL: Charles C. Thomas, 1973), p. 60.
37. Samuel Walker, *Sense and Nonsense About Crime: A Policy Guide* (Monterey, CA: Brooks/Cole, 1985), pp. 67–69.
38. J. Barry Hylton, *Safe Schools* (Boston: Butterworth-Heinemann, 1996).
39. Philip P. Purpura, *Security and Loss Prevention*, 2nd Edition (Boston: Butterworth-Heinemann, 1991); John J. Fay, *Encyclopedia of Security Management Techniques and Technology* (Boston: Butterworth-Heinemann, 1993).
40. David A. Maxwell, J.D., CPP, *Private Security Law, Case Studies* (Boston: Butterworth-Heinemann, 1993).
41. Permission obtained to reproduce from Author Christopher A. Hertig, CPP, CPO, text pending in IFPO future article, 1998.
42. Leonard Territo, James B. Halsted, and Max L. Bromley, *Crime and Justice In America: A Human Perspective*, 5th Ed. (Boston: Butterworth-Heinemann, 1998) http://www.bh.com.
43. John L. Fay, *Encyclopedia of Security Management Techniques and Technology* (Boston: Butterworth-Heinemann, 1993).
44. Ibid.
45. Leonard Territo, James B. Halsted, and Max L. Bromley, *Crime and Justice in America: A Human Perspective*, 5th Ed. (Boston: Butterworth-Heinemann, 1998) http://www.bh.com.
46. Prepared by Catherine E. Burton, Assistant Professor of Criminal Justice, Southern University.
47. Leonard Territo, James B. Halsted, and Max L. Bromley, *Crime and Justice in America: A Human Perspective*, 5th Ed. (Boston: Butterworth-Heinemann, 1998) http://www.bh.com.
48. Ibid.
49. Chris Hertig, CPP, CPO, York College, Pennsylvania.
50. David A. Maxwell, J.D., CPP, *Private Security Law, Case Studies* (Boston: Butterworth-Heinemann, 1993).

51. U.S. Department of Justice, Office of Justice Programs, Janet Reno, Attorney General, December, 1997.
52. Timothy D. Crowe, *Crime Prevention through Environmental Design* (Boston: Butterworth-Heinemann, 1991).
53. Leonard Territo, James B. Halsted, and Max L. Bromley, *Crime and Justice In America: A Human Perspective*, 5th Ed. (Boston: Butterworth-Heinemann, 1998) http://www.bh.com.
54. J. Kirk Barefoot, *Undercover Investigation*, 3rd Ed. (Boston: Butterworth-Heinemann, 1995).
55. James L. Schaub, CPP and Ken D. Biery, Jr., CPP, *Internal Theft Controls, The Ultimate Security Survey* (Boston: Butterworth-Heinemann, 1994).
56. Gerald L. Kovacich, *The Information Systems Security Officer's Guide* (Boston: Butterworth-Heinemann, 1998) http://www.bh.com.
57. Ibid.
58. Charles L. Yeschke, *The Art of Investigative Interviewing* (Boston: Butterworth-Heinemann, 1996).
59. David A. Maxwell, J.D., CPP, *Private Security Law, Case Studies* (Boston: Butterworth-Heinemann, 1993).
60. Charles L. Yeschke, *The Art of Investigative Interviewing* (Boston: Butterworth-Heinemann, 1996).
61. Ibid.
62. Ibid.
63. Ibid.
64. Ibid.
65. Ibid.
66. Ibid.
67. Ibid.
68. Charles A. Sennewald, *The Process of Investigation* (Boston: Butterworth-Heinemann, 1981).
69. Louis Tyska and Lawrence Fennelly, *150 Things You Should Know About Security* (Boston: Butterworth-Heinemann, 1998).
70. Permission obtained to reproduce *Hoffman's Detective's Tips for Business and Industry*, Volume 54, Amsterdam, Holland: Hoffman Investigation Ltd. Publications, 1998.
71. Authored by John H. Lombardi, Ph.D., CSS, CST, CPO, NAPS, IAPSC, Director of Criminal Justice Program, Southern University, Baton Rouge, Louisiana; and Russell Cook, Sr., President and CEO of Russell Cook, Sr. and Associates Investigations and Management Consulting, Baton Rouge, Louisiana.
72. Louis Tyska and Lawrence Fennelly, *150 Things You Should Know About Security* (Boston: Butterworth-Heinemann, 1998) http://www.bh.com and www.litigationconsultants.com.
73. Ibid.
74. Ibid.
75. Ibid.
76. Charles A. Sennewald, *The Process of Investigation* (Boston: Butterworth-Heinemann, 1981).
77. Leonard Territo, James B. Halsted, and Max L. Bromley, *Crime and Justice in America: A Human Perspective*, 5th Ed. (Boston: Butterworth-Heinemann, 1998) http://www.bh.com.

78. Charles A. Sennewald, *The Process of Investigation* (Boston: Butterworth-Heinemann, 1981).
79. *The American Heritage Dictionary of the English Language* (New York: Houghton Mifflin, 1969), p. 978.
80. Leonard Territo, James B. Halsted, and Max L. Bromley, *Crime and Justice In America: A Human Perspective*, 5th Ed. (Boston: Butterworth-Heinemann, 1998) http://www.bh.com.
81. Ibid.
82. Ibid.
83. Gion Green, *Introduction to Security*, 4th Ed. (Boston: Butterworth-Heinemann, 1987).
84. Michael F. Brown, *Criminal Investigations: Law and Practice* (Boston: Butterworth-Heinemann, 1998).
85. Leonard Territo, James B. Halsted, and Max L. Bromley, *Crime and Justice In America: A Human Perspective*, 5th Ed. (Boston: Butterworth-Heinemann, 1998) http://www.bh.com.
86. Charles A. Sennewald, *The Process of Investigation* (Boston: Butterworth-Heinemann, 1981).
87. Michael F. Brown, *Criminal Investigations: Law and Practice* (Boston: Butterworth-Heinemann, 1998).
88. Ibid.
89. Ibid.
90. Ibid.
91. J. Barry Hylton, *Safe Schools* (Boston: Butterworth-Heinemann, 1996).
92. Michael F. Brown, *Criminal Investigations: Law and Practice* (Boston: Butterworth-Heinemann, 1998).
93. Leonard Territo, James B. Halsted, and Max L. Bromley, *Crime and Justice In America: A Human Perspective*, 5th Ed. (Boston: Butterworth-Heinemann, 1998) http://www.bh.com.
94. Louis Tyska and Lawrence Fennelly, *150 Things You Should Know About Security* (Boston: Butterworth-Heineman, 1998) http://www.bh.com and www.litigationconsultants.com.
95. R. Scott Grasser, *FINDsomeone.com* (Boston: Butterworth-Heinemann, 1998), pp. 1, 2, 3.
96. Louis Tyska and Lawrence Fennelly, *150 Things You Should Know About Security* (Boston: Butterworth-Heineman, 1998) http://www.bh.com and www.litigationconsultants.com.
97. Michael F. Brown, *Criminal Investigations: Law and Practice* (Boston: Butterworth-Heinemann, 1998).
98. J. Kirk Barefoot, *Undercover Investigations*, 3rd Ed. (Boston: Butterworth-Heinemann, 1995).
99. Ibid.
100. Michael F. Brown, *Criminal Investigations: Law and Practice* (Boston: Butterworth-Heinemann, 1998).
101. Ibid.
102. Patrick J. Lenaghan, CPP, is with Loyal Security, Inc. Visit their Web site at www.loyalsecurity.com and www.litigationconsultants.com.

Index

Printed and bound by CPI Group (UK) Ltd, Croydon, CR0 4YY

08/05/2025

01864779-0001